COPYRIGHT©2025 by Colleen C. Carson
Cover Design by Author | Colleen Carson
Book Design by Author | Colleen Carson
Editor | Catherine Carrington

THE "MR" FACTOR Copyright © 2025
Printed in Canada/United States of America/Worldwide.
First Edition, 2025
ALL RIGHTS RESERVED. This book contains material protected under International and Federal Copyright Laws and Treaties.

ISBN   Paperback   978-1-7753176-7-8
ISBN   Electronic   978-1-7753176-8-5

DISCLAIMER:
The information contained in this book is for general informational purposes only. The author and publisher make no representations of the accuracy or completeness of any information in this book and will not be liable for any errors or omissions.

The events and conversations in this book have been set down to the best of the author's ability, although some names and details have been changed to protect the privacy of individuals. For permission requests, write to the publisher through social media. Any unauthorized reprint or use of this material is prohibited.

No part of this Book may be reproduced or transmitted in any form or by any means, electronic or mechanical, including photocopying, recording, or by any information storage and retrieval system without express wrote/written permission from the author/publisher.

AUTHOR: Colleen C. Carson

DEDICATION

"To Our Family & Friends."

"A man is like the wind. He moves fast, loud, and unpredictable. But a gentleman? He's the mountain. Steady, grounded, and unmoved by the storm. While men may chase moments, a gentleman holds presence. One passes through. The other becomes the landmark."

Colleen C. Carson

Welcome...

THE

MR

FACTOR

Carson Power Productions
Vancouver, B. C.

TABLE OF CONTENTS

6	INTRODUCTION
10	PREFACE
14	HISTORY UPDATE
25	MODERN DAY
44	INFLUENCE
48	OLIVIA IS MY NAME.
57	THE STORY OF NOAH
61	OLD STYLE
63	ART OF COMMUNICATION
77	CHIVALRY ISN'T DEAD
84	DRESS TO EXPRESS SUCCESS
98	ART OF DINING
104	ART OF INTRODUCTION
108	SOCIAL SETTINGS
113	TRAVEL ETIQUETTE
116	SELF-MASTERY
139	RELATIONSHIPS
150	ART OF ROMANCE
158	BREAKUP & REJECTION
164	MODERN DAY GENTLEMAN
170	HOW TO LEAD
177	FACTOR MOVEMENT
178	MANHOOD IS LEARNED

INTRODUCTION

THE "MR" FACTOR

Pillar One: Masters – The Monarch of Manhood

Becoming a man of depth doesn't start with what the world sees. It starts with what a man claims within. And it begins here with the Masters.

The Masters is not a title; it is a presence. He is the monarch of his mindset, the governor of his growth, and the steward of his manhood. This pillar isn't for the faint or the drifting. It's for the man who decides he will no longer be defined by his past or confined by fear. He doesn't chase control; he channels it. He doesn't silence emotion; he commands it. He doesn't react; he responds with reason, resilience, and resolve.

The Masters is a man of mental clarity and emotional composure. He owns his focus like a craftsman with a sharp and steady blade. His leadership isn't loud. It's lived in his home, in his business, and in his personal evolution. He knows that manhood is not measured by dominance but by discipline, not by noise but by nuance.

He does not bluff. He builds with intention. He does not wander. He walks with vision. He does not show up halfway. He arrives with clarity, consistency, and quiet confidence.

When a man rises into his Masters, he stops waiting for the world to grant him permission. He no longer seeks validation from outside forces. He becomes the designer of his own reality, laying down the blueprints of legacy, leadership, and lasting worth.

Pillar One is not about becoming more.

It's about becoming a Masters.

Pillar Two: Aure Chi – The Enforcer of Purpose

This is your fire. Your force. Your sacred ignition.

The Aure Chi is not a facade; it is a frequency. It doesn't posture; it pulses. It is the radiant force within every man, waiting not just to flicker but to erupt, lighting up his path with strength, honour, and unshakable purpose.

The Aure Chi is not about presence for show but presence with substance. It's walking into a room and shifting the atmosphere not with noise but with noble energy. He doesn't demand attention. He commands respect. Quietly. Powerfully.

He is the light in the darkness, the stillness in the storm, the steady flame that refuses to be extinguished. The man who embraces his Aure Chi is not fueled by ego; he is moved by mission. He doesn't run from his power; he returns to it. He doesn't seek applause; he stands in alignment.

The Aure Chi burns, but it doesn't destroy. It refines. It consumes the lies, the ones that told him he wasn't enough, the ones that tried to shrink him into a shadow of his potential. It reminds him of what he was always meant to become: a man with divine direction and unapologetic drive.

He doesn't exist to survive. He exists to set things in motion. With every step, he carries the unspoken authority of a man who knows why he's here.

Pillar Two is not about chasing purpose.

It's about becoming purpose.

Pillar Three: Nobler –The Architect of Legacy

This is where a man becomes timeless.

The Nobler is not driven by applause; he is defined by alignment. He is the mirror of legacy, the quiet architect of impact that lasts far beyond the moment. While others chase status, the Nobler builds stature not through dominance but through dignity, not through haste but through honour.

He elevates everything he touches: his words, his work, and his relationships. His thoughts rise above the surface. His choices are deliberate. His values are unshakable and etched in stone. The Nobler doesn't follow the crowd. He walks his own path with conviction, clarity, and character.

Where others react, he reflects. Where others talk, he teaches through presence, not performance. His leadership is not in the spotlight. It's in the substance. He doesn't need to be seen to be significant. He leads when no one is watching, which makes him unforgettable.

He balances ambition with integrity. Strength with softness. Confidence with humility. He is the man whose decisions earn trust and whose actions inspire emulation. He doesn't compromise his truth to move ahead. He stands for something greater because he is something greater.

The Nobler doesn't just leave a legacy. He lives it every day, in his choices and the man he chooses to be.

Pillar Three isn't about what you leave behind.

It's about what you live out. Right now.

The *"MR"* Factor: The *M*an of *R*efinement

It all builds to this: the evolution from manhood by default to manhood by design. *The "MR" Factor* isn't about being shaped by trends. It's about being sculpted by timeless truths. The *M*an of *R*efinement is not loud. He is lasting, not driven by ego but anchored in essence. He is sharp, not shallow. Bold, not brash. Gentle, never weak.

He's done the work. He's faced the mirror and didn't flinch. He's mastered himself through the steadfast stance of the Masters. He's lit his life with the bold brilliance of the Aure Chi. And he walks with the quiet power of a man whose legacy is already unfolding, the path of the Nobler.

This man doesn't need to announce his value; you feel it. He dresses like he respects himself. He speaks like he respects others. He moves like he's on a mission that matters. He's the one you want leading beside you, loving within your home, and standing in your circle. He's not chasing perfection; he's choosing presence. He's not addicted to success; he's aligned with significance. He's not living louder; he's living deeper.

And here's the truth: You don't stumble into this kind of manhood. You craft it. Day by day. Choice by choice. Thought by thought. You rise into it by living these pillars, The Masters, The Aure Chi, and The Nobler, until they're not just ideas but instincts. Until they don't just define you; they refine you.

Because when these three are alive inside you? You don't just walk into manhood. You own it. You don't just show up in the world. You shape it. That is the real power of a *M*an of *R*efinement. That is ***The "MR" Factor.***

He becomes his own Masterpiece.

PREFACE

The "MR" Factor: It's Not Fluff — It's Fire

Let's clear the smoke right now. *The "MR" Factor* isn't soft talk wrapped in scented candles and feel-good quotes. It isn't about dudes sitting in a circle crying over vision boards while sipping soy lattes. There is no shade to emotional growth, but this isn't therapy. This is transformation with edge, power with polish, and manhood redefined and refined.

This is next-level male energy. It's going from a flip phone to a full-on smartwatch. The same man, upgraded software, tighter moves, cleaner presence, and sharper vibe. We're not here to raise the volume. We're here to raise the standard.

Because the man with *The "MR" Factor* doesn't just show up, he arrives. No fireworks. No hype. Just a presence that shifts the air when he walks in. He's not loud. He's not slick. He's just that man. And everybody knows it.

It's not just about a cleaner haircut or finally retiring that cologne from your early 2000s clubbing days. It's about stepping into the Masters, igniting the Aure Chi, and embodying the Nobler. Real men don't need pick-up lines or outdated charm. They don't need cargo shorts or memes for personality. They've evolved. They're elevated.

What Is the "MR" Factor?

The "MR" Factor is the difference between trying too hard and not needing to try at all. It's not performance. It's presence. Not noise. It's notice.

It's having style with substance, charm with character, and confidence without the ego trip. He doesn't dominate the room; he defines it. He doesn't chase attention; attention finds him. And don't get it twisted: this isn't about faking confidence like some Hollywood action hero.

This is real life. This is how real men show up. *The "MR" Factor* isn't about becoming someone else. It's about becoming the most refined, powerful version of you through the three core pillars:

The Masters – Supreme mindset and self-discipline.
The Aure Chi – Purpose-driven fire and inner strength.
The Nobler – High-value living and unshakable legacy.

This man doesn't fake it. He lives it. In the way, he shakes a hand. In the way he handles pressure. In every moment, he owns.

Why It Works: Have you ever met a man with that unshakable energy? Not loud, not flashy, just solid. Everything he does feels like it matters.

His handshake? Firm, with purpose.
His eye contact? Like he's seeing you, really seeing you.
His presence? You don't just notice it; you feel it.
No cheesy pickup lines that should've died with VHS tapes.
He speaks the truth, and suddenly, people lean in.
They don't just hear him. They remember him.

That's The "MR" Factor right there.

But here's the deal: To live that level of manhood, you got to lock in eight key elements rooted deep in the Three Pillars that define a *M*an of *R*efinement.

Unlocking The "MR" Factor: **Eight Elements Rooted in the Three Pillars**

Master Your Presence (Masters)
Command, not control. Head high. Shoulders back. Grounded energy. You walk like you own your purpose, even if it's just to grab a coffee. This is the Master's zone: skill, awareness, and balance.

Own the Five Senses (Aure Chi)
People don't forget how you make them feel. Your scent, handshake texture, and the tone when you say their name are subtle but unforgettable. This is Aure Chi's heart: intentional warmth and connection.

Be Intentional with Style (Nobler)
Trends fade; style rooted in self-awareness lasts. Wear what speaks before you even say a word. Clean lines, deliberate choices. That's Nobler, with high standards in every stitch.

Speak to Connect (Masters)
Don't just fill the space with words. Communicate. Listen like you mean it. Ask questions that dig deeper. Speak with impact. The Master knows when to lead and when to hold space.

Move with Purpose (Nobler)
No fidgeting. No nervous pacing. You move like a man on a mission, not rehearsed but aligned. That's Nobler, standards in motion.

Confidence Without Ego (Aure Chi)
No need to broadcast or brag. Absolute confidence is quiet but magnetic. Aure Chi brings the heart-fueled strength that lifts others, not steps on them.

Kindness as Power (Aure Chi)
Kindness isn't a weakness. It's bold. It's decisive. It's strong and compassionate. A refined man knows how to lift people, not just impress them.

Consistency Is Key (All Three)
This is where it all comes together. Show up the same on day one or day one hundred. Build trust. Show depth. You're not a mood; you're a movement.

The Bottom Line: Let's be clear: *The "MR" Factor* isn't a costume. It's not some hype train. It's a call to evolve. This is what happens when a man decides to Master his presence, ignite the gold standard of Aure Chi, and walk tall in the Nobler way of living.

You're not just changing your clothes; you're changing your energy. Your way. Your impact. If you want to be called **MR** or **SIR**, not just out of formality but out of earned respect, this is where it begins. Because here's the truth: modern women? They don't want a performance. They want presence. They want substance. They want a man who doesn't fade after five minutes, a man who lingers in the mind and stirs the soul.

What Makes a Manhood Redefined? It's not yachts, espresso machines, or curated Insta feeds. It's not flexing. It's refining.

Manhood Redefined is power with purpose. The *"MR"* Man doesn't chase validation. He inspires respect. He doesn't need to shout. He leads. He sharpens himself until excellence is muscle memory. This isn't about tricks. This is about truth. Not pretending. Becoming. Because let's be honest: The world has enough charming fakes.

What it needs? Refined men who lead with courage. Live with character. And move through the world with unapologetic class. So, are you ready to lead with presence, live with fire, and walk like you mean it? This isn't fluff. It's FIRE. And it starts right here; With you.

HISTORY UPDATE: THE HISTORICAL EVOLUTION

Let's get something straight: *The "MR" Factor* isn't some trendy buzzword or TikTok idea. It's an evolution rooted in real history, shaped by centuries of what it truly means to be a refined man. It stands for Manhood Redefined and Male Refinement, and trust me, it's not new. It's just finally being brought back with purpose. *The "MR" Factor* is built on three unshakable pillars: Masters (your presence and purpose), Aure Chi (your heart and connection), and Nobler (your standards and style).

Back in the day, being a gentleman meant more than opening doors or wearing a three-piece suit. It was about honouring women, leading with integrity, and carrying yourself with quiet confidence. But times changed. Gender roles shifted. Relationships got more complex. And yet, the real definition of a gentleman didn't disappear. It just leveled up.

Today, *The "MR" Factor* is how a modern man shows up in life, not just in love but in every interaction. It's how he listens, speaks, respects others, and, most importantly, respects himself. This isn't about nostalgia. It's about revival.

And these three pillars, Masters, Aure Chi, and Nobler, aren't optional. They're your foundation. Because here's the truth: the world doesn't need more loud talkers or smooth players. It needs men who move with depth, lead with honour, and make a presence of their power. *The "MR" Factor* isn't about keeping up. It's about rising up.

Medieval Era: The Birth of Chivalry (5th – 15th Century)

In the medieval period, the concept of a 'gentleman' was intricately linked to the esteemed feudal nobility and the code of chivalry. The knights, not just for their noble bloodlines but for the ideals they embodied, became the cornerstone of what we now understand as 'gentlemanly conduct.' It wasn't just about the sword in hand, but the integrity in the heart. Knights were expected to be warriors, but the accurate measure of their manhood was in how they conducted themselves when the battle was over.

It was about understanding that true strength wasn't in brute force but in how you protected, guided, and uplifted others, especially those who were vulnerable or of lower status. This included women, who were often seen as needing protection and guidance, and the knights' treatment of them was a key aspect of their chivalrous conduct.

A sense of maturity is at the core of *The "MR" Factor*. Knights weren't young, hot-headed men seeking glory; they were seasoned warriors who bore responsibility like a weight on their shoulders. It wasn't just about wielding a sword or charging into battle; it was about handling adversity with grace, making wise decisions, and leading with steadfast honour. They were warriors and symbols of strength, compassion, and responsibility. They embodied what it meant to be a man who could stand tall in battle and life.

Over time, the essence of a true man, as defined by *The "MR" Factor,* evolved. In medieval times, the substance of a true man wasn't found in power or privilege but in the integrity of his actions, the nobility of his heart, and the courage of his character. These were the pillars that shaped the gentleman long before we even knew the term. Today, the concept of a gentleman has evolved, but its core values of integrity, nobility, and courage still resonate in our modern notions of masculinity.

Renaissance Era: The Rise of the Aristocrat

Fast-forward to the Renaissance, and the idea of being a gentleman was significantly refined. This period introduced courtly love, where men weren't just expected to be tough in battle; they needed to be smooth in conversation, refined in their actions, and respectful in private and public life. *The "MR" Factor*, a term coined to represent the multifaceted qualities of a gentleman, starts to evolve.

A man's worth wasn't just about physical prowess but about how well he carried himself in all situations. He needed to demonstrate maturity, be respectful, and possess the quiet confidence that comes from knowing his worth without needing to boast about it. This is where the gentleman, as we know him, starts to come into focus: someone who balances strength with grace and humility.

The term 'gentleman' undergoes a significant transformation during this period. It expands its scope to include not only warriors and landowners, but also those who do not toil the land and can afford to concentrate on refining themselves and their estates. The English gentry emerges as a potent societal force, ushering in a new class.

With this newfound status, there is a heightened emphasis on civility, manners, and proper behaviour. Gentlemen are now expected to adhere to a new standard of conduct that transcends physical strength or material success; it is about how one carries oneself in the world. This entails understanding the importance of respecting others, traditions, and the social codes that govern human interaction.

Education takes center stage in defining the true gentleman as we transition into the Renaissance and early modern period. Humanism and the pursuit of knowledge are no longer optional but integral to a man's identity. Gentlemen are expected to be well-read, articulate, and capable of engaging in meaningful conversations.

However, this is not about flaunting knowledge but contributing to discussions with wisdom and tact. A gentleman's education becomes as crucial as his social skills as the Renaissance ideal broadens to encompass cultural sophistication. Courtly behaviour, such as active participation in the cultural life of the court, becomes a key indicator of status.

Then, the enlightenment came along and shifted the idea of masculinity again. The Age of Enlightenment pushed for reason, intellectualism, and rational discourse. It's no longer enough to be a gentleman physically; now, a man is expected to have a sharp mind, be well-versed in literature and philosophy, and articulate his thoughts with respect for others.

The salons, elegant drawing rooms where polite conversation and intellectual discussion were the primary forms of entertainment, and coffeehouses, public social spaces where people gathered to discuss literature, politics, and philosophy, became popular gathering spots for these intellectual conversations. Being a gentleman now means engaging in polite, respectful discussions where everyone's opinion holds value.

Maturity has become a key factor here, too. The Renaissance gentleman is no longer just a warrior; he's a cultured man refined in thought and action. Respect evolves from being about physical prowess or social status to being about social grace and the ability to conduct oneself with dignity in all situations. Whether in the court or at the local tavern, a gentleman knows how to navigate the world with poise, earning respect not through force but through intellect, manners, and how he treats others.

Victorian Era: 19th Century: The Victorian Gentleman

The Victorian Era, spanning the 19th century, is when the concept of the "gentleman" began to take on a more formal shape. Society demanded more from men, especially regarding their morals and behaviour. The Victorian gentleman wasn't just looking sharp and having good manners.

He was expected to embody high moral standards, integrity, responsibility, and an almost palpable sense of respectability. Being wealthy or well-connected wasn't enough; being a true gentleman meant living by ethical principles that positively reflected the individual and society.

As the Industrial Revolution changed the landscape, the idea of being a gentleman also evolved. It started to include professionals, doctors, lawyers, and clergymen, those men who were respected in their fields and expected to be pillars of moral fortitude. The Victorian gentleman didn't just work hard; he worked with purpose. There was an idea that success wasn't only about wealth, but also about how much you gave back.

A gentleman was often involved in social reform, giving time and money to causes that bettered society. For instance, they might have been involved in campaigns for better working conditions, education for the underprivileged, or healthcare for the poor. Philanthropy became a mark of distinction. The more a man contributed to the common good, the more he embodied the true essence of gentlemanliness.

Let's examine the Victorian values that solidified *The "MR" Factor* in public perception. Respect, manners, and decorum were not mere social etiquette but reflections of one's character. How you treated others, conducted yourself in society, and interacted with women mattered. These actions were intricately tied to your reputation and your position in the social hierarchy.

Regarding family, respect for women and protecting family honour were non-negotiable. A gentleman was expected to be the provider, the protector, and the firm support of his family and society.

Maturity during this time was about more than age or experience; it was about responsibility. The Victorian gentleman was expected to have a stable career, maintain family love and honour, and stick to society's norms. This wasn't just about personal achievement but about fulfilling your role in the greater societal machine while maintaining that sense of dignity and decorum.

In the Victorian sense, respect was also about following strict social codes. There were rules for everything: how you dressed (formal attire was a must, especially in public), how you spoke (politeness and eloquence were highly valued), how you treated women (with utmost respect and chivalry), and even how you moved through public spaces (with grace and dignity).

Public conduct was paramount. A gentleman didn't just act with dignity; he radiated it. He knew when to speak, when to stay silent, when to bow his head, and when to step forward. Politeness wasn't optional; it was essential.

The Victorian gentleman was a man of humility who understood that true strength wasn't about flexing power but about demonstrating grace in all situations. This era of formal etiquette and social propriety marked a defining moment in the evolution of gentlemanliness, one where respect for others and adherence to social codes weren't just expectations; they were the very foundation of being a man.

Modern Era: Early 20th Century: Redefining the Gentleman

The early 20th century marked a massive transformation, not just in society but in the essence of what it meant to be a gentleman. World wars shook up old notions of class and privilege. Suddenly, heroism and the willingness to serve your country became new standards that made a man respectable, an early demonstration of what we now call the Masters Pillar: presence, responsibility, and purpose under pressure.

The traditional idea of a gentleman, once tied to wealth and aristocracy, began to shift. It wasn't about bloodlines but the qualities you brought courage, selflessness, and a willingness to rise to the occasion. The Nobler Pillar emerged in spirit: setting high personal standards and choosing refinement over entitlement.

The "MR" Factor, means that any man can personify a gentleman's qualities, regardless of their background. It's less about where you came from and more about how you carried yourself in the world, a balance of the three pillars, especially the Aure Chi Pillar, which called for genuine heart, emotional intelligence, and deeper connection with others.

Industrialization and urbanization introduced new challenges to traditional notions of masculinity. The rise of cities and factories and changes in class structures meant that the old ways were rapidly becoming outdated. Yet, through all these shifts, the core of what made a man a gentleman, *The "MR" Factor*, remained intact. A man's Mastery of himself, the refinement of his choices, and the warmth of his spirit defined him.

It wasn't about what you owned or where you lived; it was about how you treated others, the dignity with which you carried yourself, and how you adapted to the changing world while still holding on to your values.

One of the most significant cultural shifts during this time was the rise of women's rights and the increasing social mobility across all classes. As women gained more independence, the concept of respect also began to evolve. No longer was respect about protecting women as fragile creatures; it was about treating them as equals. The Aure Chi Pillar came alive here, encouraging men to lead with empathy, humility, and heart-centered respect.

Maturity, too, started to take on a deeper meaning. It wasn't just about age or experience; it was about emotional intelligence and personal integrity. A modern gentleman could handle life's pressures without losing his cool, understand his emotions, and be afraid to show vulnerability when necessary. This is the very embodiment of the Masters Pillar self-command rooted in authenticity.

Respect became much more nuanced during this period. Instead of following social codes and doing what was expected, it was about treating everyone with kindness and consideration, regardless of their background or status. Respect wasn't reserved for the powerful; it was something to be earned and given freely to all, a true reflection of the Nobler Pillar, where honour is chosen, not inherited.

Emerging gender roles, shifting societal expectations, and new cultural values led to respect evolving from a formal notion to something more personal, deeper, and rooted in genuine equality.

Throughout these changes, the early 20th century marked a pivotal moment when traditional manners merged with modern sensibilities, giving rise to a new understanding of what it meant to be a gentleman. It was no longer about looking good on paper or following outdated norms.

It was about being a man who could adapt, respect others, and embrace the changing world while still holding onto timeless values of integrity, courage, and emotional strength. The gentleman of the modern era was a man grounded in Masters, guided by Aure Chi, and committed to living Nobler. And that, at its core, is *The "MR" Factor.*

Late 20th Century to Present: The Modern Gentleman

The old-school definitions of class, wealth, or race no longer apply to today's modern gentleman. Instead, he's all about the core qualities that define a proper man: integrity, respect, and social responsibility.

In a world where inclusivity and diversity are front and center, being a gentleman is less about fitting into a mold and more about shaping yourself to be the best version of who you are, and treating everyone around you with dignity, no matter their background. His adaptability in a changing world is truly inspiring.

Regarding gender equality, the modern gentleman understands that respect is mutual. Gone are the days of traditional roles where men had to protect or provide for women in a patronizing sense. Today, respect for women, gender equality, and people's choices is the foundation of being a truly respectful man. It's not about taking the lead by default but lifting others, regardless of gender, and standing alongside them.

Maturity today isn't just about the number of years you've been alive; it's about emotional intelligence and self-awareness. It's about knowing yourself well enough to form deep, meaningful relationships and showing empathy towards those, you care about. The modern gentleman's emotional intelligence ensures that everyone feels understood and respected. Modern maturity is about knowing when to speak up and when to listen, and it involves recognizing that strength often comes from vulnerability. It's essential to understand that emotional growth is just as significant as professional success.

Respect has taken on a broader meaning in the 21st century. It's not confined to those in positions of power, nor is it about following outdated social hierarchies. Respect today is about acknowledging everyone's autonomy and boundaries. It's about embracing diverse perspectives, whether that's through cultural differences or new ways of thinking. The modern gentleman listens attentively and is slow to judge, valuing the voices of others and making everyone feel included and valued.

The feminist movements and the evolution of gender roles have reshaped what it means to be a man. Strength is no longer tied to dominance. Strength is measured by empathy, understanding, respecting boundaries, and the emotional intelligence to navigate romantic, familial, or professional relationships. The modern gentleman isn't afraid to show respect for consent, boundaries, and emotional well-being.

Globalization and the increasing diversity of cultures and beliefs mean that a gentleman today must be even more adaptable and respectful. It's not enough to tolerate differences; the modern gentleman actively seeks to learn about others' backgrounds, understand what drives them, and honour their perspectives. In a multicultural society, being a gentleman means treating every person, regardless of their background, with the same respect and dignity you would expect for yourself.

With the rise of the digital age, manners have expanded beyond the physical world into online spaces. How you behave in person is essential, but how you present yourself online is equally vital. A true gentleman today knows that social media isn't a free-for-all to disrespect others. Politeness, punctuality, and courtesy are just as necessary in digital interactions as they are in face-to-face interactions. Respecting others' privacy and avoiding the temptation to tear people down for clicks or likes are now part of what it means to be a modern man.

So, what does *The "MR" Factor* look like today? It's an evolving blend of traditional values and modern sensibilities. It's about knowing when to stand firm in your beliefs and when to adapt to new understandings of what it means to be a respectful man. Maturity today is about emotional resilience and engaging in open, honest conversations. Manners extend to every interaction, whether in person or online.

Respect has evolved into a multifaceted understanding of autonomy, boundaries, and empathy. In a rapidly changing world, the modern gentleman knows that being a good man is a lifelong journey defined by continual growth, awareness, and respect for the diverse world around him.

THE MODERN DAY "MR" FACTOR

Today's idea of what makes a gentleman has evolved with the times. It's a mix of old-school virtues that have stood the test of time, but with a modern twist that reflects our world. *The "MR" Factor* isn't stuck in the past; it's about a man who knows how to adapt, grow, and do right by others, no matter the situation.

Maturity (Masters):
In the modern world, maturity is no longer just about having a full beard or owning a house. It's about emotional intelligence, the ability to read the room, understand other people's feelings, and remain calm when things get tough. It's about flexibility, being able to bounce back when life throws a punch, and not just surviving but thriving through adversity. A real man knows how to communicate openly, honestly, and respectfully. It's about listening more than talking; when you speak, it's with thoughtfulness and intention.

Manners (Aure Chi):
Being a modern gentleman means understanding that manners aren't just for dinner parties; they're a way of life. Whether you're face-to-face or behind a screen, how you treat people matters. Politeness, punctuality, and courtesy go a long way. It's not about putting on a front or following rigid social rules; it's about treating others with dignity, whether you're shaking someone's hand, sending an email, or commenting in a discussion. A gentleman knows that small acts of respect, like saying "please" and "thank you," still go a long way, and it's not just a matter of habit; it's a matter of character.

Respect (Nobler):
In today's world, respect is more thoughtful than following the "treat others how you want to be treated" mantra. It's about understanding boundaries, recognizing people's experiences,

and valuing those differences. It's about empathy, putting yourself in someone else's shoes and seeing the world through their eyes. Being a gentleman means giving others the space to be themselves, listening without judgment, and valuing their opinions, even when they differ from your own.

It's not about always agreeing; it's about creating an environment where people feel seen and heard. *The "MR" Factor* still stands tall in a constantly shifting world. It's not about perfection; it's about striving to be better, to lead with heart, and to respect humanity in everyone. That's what makes a modern man a gentleman in today's world.

In conclusion, *The "MR" Factor* has always been central to being a gentleman, stretching centuries of shifting social norms and expectations. From the knights of medieval chivalry to today's modern man, these core pillars have constantly evolved to keep pace with the changing world.

But at the heart of it, being a gentleman isn't just about bowing to tradition or following old-school rules; it's about exemplifying qualities like emotional intelligence, gender equality, and a deep respect for others.

The role of emotional intelligence in the modern gentleman is crucial, as it allows for better understanding and management of one's own emotions and those of others, leading to more effective communication and interpersonal relationships.

As times have changed, so has the definition of a gentleman. In medieval times, it was all about protecting the weak and displaying courage in battle. Fast forward to the modern era, and we see that being a gentleman is far broader; it's about equality, empathy, and genuine consideration for those around you.

Empathy, in particular, plays a significant role in the modern gentleman, as it allows for a deeper understanding of others' perspectives and feelings, fostering better relationships and a more inclusive society.

Yet, throughout this evolution, the essential values of maturity and respect have never wavered. These values aren't just relics of the past; they're living, breathing principles that still matter today. Now, let's discuss a missing ingredient in modern men: we call it romance.

Modern relationships have lost something significant in a world driven by fast-paced lifestyles, instant gratification, and digital interactions. It's not love, for love still exists in many forms. It's not attraction, for men and women still seek connection. It's something deeper, something essential, that used to set apart the ordinary from the extraordinary - the art of romance. The absence of this art leaves a void, a longing for the days when romance was a defining element of relationships.

Romance, the timeless bridge between affection and passion, has become the missing ingredient in modern men. Once the defining trait of gentlemen, it has been replaced by complacency, confusion, indifference and sometimes just pure laziness.

But here's the deal: romance isn't outdated, unnecessary, or reserved for special occasions. It is the secret weapon of the unforgettable man, the one who not only loves but also leaves a lasting impression.

Colleen: Romance didn't just pack its bags and leave one day. It faded... slowly. And a big reason? Convenience. These days, everything's instant. A heart emoji, a flower order, or a dinner reservation are all done with a few taps on a screen. Don't get me wrong, technology makes things easier, but it also waters things down.

Donald: She's right. Just because you can send a rose emoji doesn't mean you should stop putting in real effort. Real romance takes time. It takes thought. It's not about clicking "send". It's about making her feel seen.

Colleen: There was a time when men wrote love letters. They sat down, put pen to paper, and poured out their hearts. And guess what? Remember, Babe, you did that for me. One Christmas, he gave me a handwritten letter. No gift has ever touched me like that one. That's what romance looks like.

Donald: I wasn't trying to be old-fashioned. I was just being real. That letter? It came from my heart. Sometimes, the most powerful thing a man can do is slow down, look at his woman, and say, "You matter. Let me show you."

Colleen: Somewhere along the way, society decided romance made a man soft. Like if he expressed love, he lost his edge. But that's not true. The strongest men, the kings, the poets, the warriors, they didn't hold back. Romance wasn't weakness; it was devotion.

Donald: Exactly. Loving deeply doesn't make you less of a man. It makes you more. Real men know their value, and they offer it to a woman who values them right back. That's not surrender; that's soul-level strength.

Colleen: Look around across movies, romance books, and once-upon-a-times. The romantic is often the warrior. Not because he wields a sword. But because he dares to feel deeply. To fight for connection in a world that too often tells him not to. He is brave not only in battle but also in love, loyalty, and vulnerability. Take a look at the greats: Colin Firth in Love Actually, Ryan Gosling in The Notebook, and Richard Gere in Pretty Woman.

Donald: And sure, times have changed. Women today are strong, independent, and self-made. And that's something to celebrate. But too many men saw that and thought, "Well, I guess romance isn't needed anymore." Wrong move.

Colleen: Romance was never about control or outdated roles. It's about connection. It's about making a woman feel chosen. A confident woman doesn't need romance. She wants a man who understands that it's not about need; it's about desire, a significant difference. Go ahead, reread that line.

Donald: I heard that loud and clear. Romance isn't about rescuing her; it's about wanting her. Showing up because you choose her every day, not because you think she can't handle life on her own.

Colleen: Romance breathes in the slow moments. The lingering glances. The handwritten notes. Those long talks that stretch until early morning. That's what builds connection. But let's be honest, today's dating scene is in a hurry. Swipe, text, move on. It's lost its patience.

Donald: And patience? It's not optional. It's everything. Romance isn't some instant gratification game. It's not fast food; it's a slow, intentional meal rich with flavour, meaning, and presence. You have to take your time, listen, learn, and linger in the moment. But here's the truth: some people still think they can bypass all that and still end up with something real.

They're wrong. Because if you skip the romance, what you're left with isn't a connection, just a convenience. Let's be honest: it wasn't about you. She just needed something in that moment, and you were available. That's not chemistry. That's circumstance.

Colleen: Ask any woman, especially the divorced ones, and they'll tell you romance matters. It's not extra. It's the oxygen that keeps the fire burning. It's what separates "just a man" from her man.

Donald: Anybody can shoot off a "Good morning, beautiful" text. That's easy. But being the reason, she feels beautiful? That's a whole different game. That's *The "MR" Factor.* And that guy, the one who brings the fire, the depth, and the heart? He's unforgettable.

Colleen: Like I said in The Guyed Book, "Romance is the thank you in love." And that still holds true. Because real romance isn't loud, it's intentional. It's the quiet acknowledgment that says, "I see you. I value you. Thank you for choosing me." It's in the patience, the effort, and the small, meaningful acts. Romance is gratitude in motion, where love stops being assumed and starts being appreciated.

Donald: Did you get that? *"Romance is the thank you in love."* Now, let that sink in. Romance isn't just roses and reservations. It's how you show you're grateful to have her in your life. It's saying, "Thanks for loving me." Without actually saying it. And if you're skipping that part? You're not loving; you're just coasting. A real gentleman never forgets to thank love for showing up.

Colleen: Many men think romance is something they do for women like it's some item to check off the list. But let me tell you what I learned when I rewrote my first book. I signed up on eight online dating sites to understand romance from a man's perspective.

Yep, eight. I had to move fast with my research, like speed research. I met with over a hundred men for coffee, lunch, and sometimes dinner, honest conversations with real guys who eventually figured out I was interviewing them for my book, The Guyed Book (yep, that's "guyed," not "guide' second meaning" guy ed").

Every single time, I asked the same question: Are you romantic? Not one man said no. Not even a maybe. I mean, they lit up like Christmas lights. "Of course I am!" Some were practically ready to beat their chest like Tarzan. Confidence? Off the charts. So, then I'd ask the follow-up: Describe a romantic evening with a beautiful woman.

Boom. Cue the greatest hits: Candlelit Dinner, One Red Rose, Barefoot Walks on the Beach, and Moonlight Strolls. It was like they all read the same script from a 90s rom-com. They all said the same things as if reading from the same script.

Donald: Let me get this, Sweetheart. Now listen up, guys, because this part matters: Let me say it louder for the guys in the back: All. Women. Are. Not. The. Same. Romance isn't one-size-fits-all.

It's not about recycled gestures or Hollywood moments. It's about knowing her. What lights her up? It's about learning her. What makes her feel seen, special, and safe? That's the real stuff. Creating something that feels true between the two of you. That's the kind of romance that sticks.

So, if you're out here thinking you've got the whole 'romantic man' thing down because you've mastered dinner and a rose, maybe it's time to go deeper. Real romance isn't something you do for a woman; it's something you create with her. Real romance doesn't live in clichés. It lives in connection. And the moment you understand that?

Colleen: That's when the sparks stop being cliché and start becoming unforgettable. The truth is, romancing a woman also strengthens a man. It teaches him the power of attentiveness, the art of communication, and the confidence of knowing that he can make a woman feel special. A man who masters romance isn't just more attractive to women; he's more appealing to himself.

Donald: Any guy can pull out his wallet, but a real gentleman who personifies *The "MR" Factor* opens his heart and mind. Romance isn't about how much you spend; it's about the effort, creativity, and genuine thoughtfulness you put into it. A man who understands that? He's in a league of his own.

Colleen: And here's the good news: romance isn't dead; it's just waiting for someone bold enough to return it. Any man can step up and make it happen. It doesn't take grand gestures or extravagant spending. A simple note on her pillow, a heartfelt compliment, or a surprise coffee delivery says more than money ever could.

Donald: Guys, it's about the little things that show she's on your mind, a quick midday call to say, "I love you," or sending her a love song with a text that says, "Been thinking of you." That's romance. That's effort. That's how you make her feel truly special. Are you getting it now?

Colleen: Words matter more than you think. A man who speaks with intent, warmth, and sincerity can create a world of romance without spending a single dime. It's not just about throwing out compliments; it's about making her feel truly seen. Admiration is nice, but understanding? That's where the magic is, right Babe?

Donald: Absolutely. And when you're with her, be with her. Please turn off the football game, trust me, it won't keep you warm at night. Put the iPhone down. Look into her eyes. Listen. Make her feel like, in that moment, nothing else exists but her. That's romance.

Anniversaries and birthdays? Sure, those are expected. But real romance happens in everyday moments, the random Tuesday when you send flowers for no reason, the Friday morning when you make her coffee just as she likes, and the moment you lean in and whisper, "I appreciate you." Surprise her when she least expects it because that's when it means the most.

Colleen: Too many men start strong and fade over time. But the secret of legendary romance? It evolves. How you romanced her initially isn't the same as how you'll romance her after years together. The effort must grow, not disappear. Romance isn't about grand gestures or poetry but intention, presence, and effort.

Donald: It's about making a woman feel like she's worth the time, the thought, and the little things that make love extraordinary. So, to every man who has ever thought romance doesn't matter anymore, think again. It's the missing ingredient in modern men and the one thing that will set you apart: *The "MR" Factor* knows romance is not dead. It's just waiting for the right man to revive it.

In a world where social expectations are constantly shifting, *The "MR" Factor* remains constant. It reminds us that, no matter how much society changes, certain values, such as the importance of treating others with dignity and respect, will always be fundamental to being a true gentleman.

Colleen: As a reader, you are an integral part of this concept, and your value in upholding these principles cannot be overstated. As we move forward, the definition of being a gentleman will continue to adapt. Still, the core pillars of Masters, Aure Chi, and Nobler will always stand the test of time, inspiring us with their spirit.

Alright, now you've got the lowdown on the history of a gentleman and the scoop on *The "MR" Factor*. Pretty sweet, right? History deserves its props, but new ideas. They should be welcomed with open arms. After all, that's what keeps the world spinning. Don't you think? Alright, let's have an honest talk.

So, you've probably heard the term "gentleman" tossed around here and there, but what does it mean in today's world? Many people think it's all about wearing a suit and being polished, but let me tell you, being a true gentleman goes way deeper than just looking good. It's about living with principles that help you be better for yourself and the people around you.

Here's the deal: it's about sincerity, style, and success, not the kind of success that's all about money and fancy titles, but the kind that makes you feel proud of who you are and how you show up in the world. It's all about being true to yourself and doing the right thing.

Donald: Sincerity, my friends, is the cornerstone. In a world where fake smiles and superficial conversations prevail, being genuine is a breath of fresh air. When you're real with people, they notice. They respect it. It's one of the most essential things a gentleman can offer. If you say you'll do something, you do it. No excuses. And if you mess up? Own it. Acknowledge it, learn from it, and keep moving forward. It's as simple as that. This sincerity builds trust and respect, the foundation of every solid relationship.

Colleen: Oh, we women notice, I assure you. And let me tell you, the fakeness? It's glaring. I have to mention this fakeness comes in all genders. But here's the good news: You can change that. It's almost impressive how exhausting it is, but you don't have to keep it up. And if you think that shallow act of yours got her into bed faster, think again. If you think you pulled that off, newsflash: you didn't. You got played. She needed sex, and you were just the perfect setup.

When you're sincere, people trust you. Trust is the foundation of every solid relationship, whether with friends, family, or colleagues at work. People appreciate honesty and realness. No one wants to deal with someone who says one thing and does another. So, if you want to build meaningful connections, start with sincerity. It's the most solid foundation you can have.

Donald: Now, let's talk about style in terms of how you present and carry yourself. A true gentleman understands his looks reflect his feelings about himself. It doesn't matter if he's rocking a T-shirt, jeans, or a sharp, tailored suit; honestly, I'm into both, but they've got their moments. The key is feeling comfortable and confident in whatever you're wearing. Just own it!

Style, my friends, it's not about being flashy; it's about being thoughtful and showing respect. When you look good, feel good, and treat others with respect, you convey a great deal without saying a word. This style, this respect, earns you confidence and respect in return.

Okay, let's talk about something near and not so dear to my heart: your suits. Honestly, I've seen some of you strutting around in suits that look like you borrowed them from your little brother because yours was still at the cleaners.

Or worse, you rolled out of bed after a night out with the boys and thought, "Eh, this shirt from the laundry basket should do." Brace yourself: It does not do. And can we talk about the tight suit trend for a second? Those super skinny pants and jackets so short they look like they lost the rest of the fabric in a fashion tragedy?

Listen, you're not fooling anybody. You look like Mommy accidentally washed your suit on hot and now you're playing dress-up in a shrunken version of manhood. Look, I don't care what the runway says. If you can't bend your knees or lift your arms without something popping, you're not wearing a suit, you're surviving in one. Be a man. Dress like one. Tailored, confident, grown-up.

Colleen: Because believe me when I say this loud and clear: Women want a man, not a boy, trying to pass for one in a baby-sized blazer. Then, there's success. But let's be clear: it's not the kind you're probably thinking of. It's not just about climbing the corporate ladder or filling your bank account, though I understand why you might think that, especially in a place like Vancouver.

Donald: Success is about being proud of who you are, what you do, and how you help others. A true gentleman is someone who not only focuses on his growth but also lifts others. The journey of personal growth is not just a part of being a gentleman; it's the core of it. Helping someone else succeed doesn't take anything away from your journey; it only improves it.

Colleen: Success also means growing daily, whether in your personal life, career, or just as a human being. If you're not learning or improving, what's the point? A gentleman is continually striving to improve. And not just for the sake of it, but because he knows that becoming the best version of himself improves everything around him.

So, here's how you can start living like this right now: Be honest. If you say you'll do something, do it. If you make a mistake, don't be afraid to admit it and move forward. People respect you way more when you're straight with them. It's not always easy, but it's worth it. Treat everyone with respect, not just the boss or your date, but everyone.

The waiter, the person you bump into on the street, as Canadians, we're always polite; we always apologize, even when we bump into you and your friends, your family. Respect is the easiest way to show people you value them. And trust me, it goes a long way.

Donald: Here's some solid advice: listen more than you talk. Seriously. God gave us two ears and one mouth for a reason, so shut up and listen! People love feeling heard, and guess what? You don't always need to have the perfect answer. Sometimes, just being a good listener speaks volumes about your character.

Colleen: And guys, here's a tip: Listen when your woman's going off about something bothering her. If she wants your opinion, she'll ask for it. Trust me, sometimes all we need is a shoulder to cry on, not a lecture.

This act of listening, of understanding, is what makes you empathetic and trustworthy. Take care of your appearance, but don't stress about being perfect. Let's be real: Perfect isn't a thing. But you can be imperfectly perfect, and that's way more attractive. It's about putting in a little effort. There's no need to break the bank on a new wardrobe, but a little thought goes a long way.

I remember this man I met; he was charming. The first time I saw him, he was wearing a long black raincoat with a cool hat, and I have to admit, he looked good. So, I was excited when he asked me for dinner the next night. It took me two hours to prepare, and I picked the perfect outfit. I wanted to impress, and I felt beautiful.

He picked me up in the same outfit from the day before: the same coat, hat, everything. We went for a walk along the seawall, had dinner, and at the end of the night, he walked me to my door and asked if he could see me again.

I said no. He looked utterly thrown off, as if I had just told him his dog had run away. When he asked why, I told him straight up: I put effort into how I wanted to present myself, and you, well, you did absolutely nothing. And if you're this lazy in the early stages of dating, I can only imagine how bad six months down the road would be. So, yeah. There you go. Please dress for the occasion, but don't overdo it.

Donald: Honestly? I'm grateful that guy did what he did because if he hadn't, you and I might have never crossed paths. Sometimes, what looks like a loss is just life making room for something better.

Now, real quick confidence. It's magnetic. Walk like you've got a purpose, speak like you mean it, and people will pay attention. But don't cross the line into arrogance. Nobody's impressed by ego. Confidence whispers, "I got this." Arrogance shouts, "Look at me!" The gentleman? He shows up, does his thing, and lets his presence speak for itself.

Colleen: Let your actions speak louder than your words. Keep growing. Success isn't about a destination; it's a journey. Keep learning, improving, and striving to improve every day. Whether you acquire new skills, read a book, or reflect on your actions, growth is essential to success.

Donald: Last but not least, help others. You don't have to be a superhero to make an impact. Share your knowledge, offer a helping hand, and encourage others to succeed. A true gentleman knows that the world is better when everyone rises together. So, what does all this boil down to? It's not about perfection, not about being someone you're not.

It's about being real, showing up as your best self, and treating others with respect. It's about living purposefully and letting your actions speak louder than anything else. If you want to be the person who stands out for all the right reasons, start living with sincerity, accepting your style, and focusing on success. That's more than just what's in your bank account.

The idea of a gentleman has evolved. It's no longer about adhering to formal rules and codes, though those still matter. Being a gentleman is about personal growth. It's about continuously improving your emotional intelligence, communication, and character.

Colleen: Gentlemen today have to be more than just chivalrous. They must also be emotionally available, open to vulnerability, and self-aware. This journey of personal growth is what makes the modern gentleman truly inspiring.

This isn't the 1950s, when the word "gentleman" was associated with simple gestures, such as knowing how to dance at a gala or holding a cigar with elegance. Back then, a gentleman like my Dad carried a quiet elegance, moving with a calm dignity that spoke louder than words.

He communicated with respect, and his life was a testament to integrity. When he entered a dining establishment or any place, he was always addressed as *"MR"* or "**Sir**". That simple acknowledgment - *MR* - was a mark of something deeper, something earned.

The "MR" Factor, as it's now called, is a concept that I saw take shape in my own life from the example set by my Dad. It's a part of who I am, shaped by the steady, honourable man who raised me. But today, *The "MR" Factor* carries a different weight. It's not just about the external display of manners or appearances. Today, it's about being a leader in relationships, understanding the complexities of respect, and navigating life's challenges with the same quiet integrity that was once second nature.

Donald: *The "MR" Factor* is a mindset that encourages a never-ending journey of self-improvement. It calls for guys to rise above to exemplify values beyond surface-level chivalry. It asks them to challenge themselves daily, to stand as pillars of reliability, honesty, and respect.

And when those rare few exemplify the true core of The "MR" Factor walk into a room, they are addressed as *Mr.* or *Sir*. These titles carry a certain weight, a recognition that their integrity and character have been earned, not given.

Colleen: It's a bittersweet truth real gentlemen have become rare gems in today's world. But then, there's you, Donald. You embody everything *The "MR" Factor* stands for. A true gentleman in every sense, gracious, grounded, and worthy of being called Mr. or Sir wherever you go. And the best part? You're all mine.

It's no secret that communication is everything. Whether expressing your thoughts clearly, listening intently, or engaging in meaningful conversations, *The "MR" Factor* emphasizes the importance of mastering communication. Gone are the days of silent, stoic men who communicate only through gestures or brief words.

The modern gentleman must recognize that communication is an art. He must know when to speak, how to listen, and, most importantly, how to show up for others through his words and actions. By mastering the art of communication, you can cultivate more meaningful connections and deeper understanding in your relationships.

Donald: A gentleman's words are his bond. *The "MR" Factor* encourages men to think before they speak, to say what they mean, and to mean what they say. In relationships, communication can make or break the connection. A gentleman knows this, and he makes it a priority to cultivate healthy, open communication. Chivalry isn't dead; it's just evolved.

The "MR" Factor modernizes chivalry by expanding it beyond the traditional expectations of opening doors and pulling out chairs. Those acts are still charming, but chivalrous today means showing kindness, consideration, and respect in every situation.

Colleen: For example, a modern gentleman doesn't treat a woman well simply out of obligation; he does it because he sees her as his equal. *The "MR" Factor* calls for equality, mutual respect, and shared experiences. It's about lifting one another and breaking free from outdated gender roles.

I can't help but reflect on my Dad, who always viewed my Mom as his equal and repeatedly reminded his daughters that we were just as worthy as any man. He ensured we knew that, and though I can't speak for my sisters, I've never forgotten those words. I've lived by them and carried them through life, even as the world drifted further from that simple truth.

The "MR" Factor is crucial in challenging outdated notions of masculinity. It encourages men to welcome their full range of emotions, acknowledge vulnerability, and step away from the idea that they must constantly "be tough." Toxic masculinity teaches men to suppress their feelings, to avoid showing weakness, and to compete at all costs.

Donald: A gentleman who personifies *The "MR" Factor* flips this. It's about celebrating authenticity, nurturing meaningful relationships, and fostering emotional growth. In this sense, a gentleman doesn't stifle his feelings or avoid conflict; he faces challenges head-on with emotional intelligence and grace.

What does *The "MR" Factor* look like in action? Well, it's a lot of things. The man sends a thoughtful message when he knows someone's having a rough day. It's the man who listens with his full attention when a friend is pouring their heart out. It's the man who admits when he's wrong and works to make things right. It's the man who chooses kindness over ego, supports others without expecting anything in return, and strives for self-improvement every day.

Colleen: Let me take a moment to reflect on chivalry not as a relic of the past but as a living legacy of romance rooted in maturity, manners, and respect. True chivalry in today's world stands firm on three timeless pillars: Masters, Aure Chi, and Nobler. These aren't abstract ideals. They are the soul-prints of the modern gentleman, the foundation of his refined approach to love.

Donald: I used to think romance was about sweeping gestures, roses, dinners, and grand declarations. But now? I've learned it starts with me. If I can't master myself, I'll never be able to love someone else well. Chivalry isn't about pretending to be perfect. It's about showing up with presence, consistency, and genuine respect.

Colleen: A gentleman who embodies the Masters within himself understands that romantic connection begins long before he offers his heart to someone else. It begins with self-respect, emotional discipline, and a clear purpose. He doesn't dive into romance fueled by charm or impulse. He approaches it with clarity and care, creating a space where his partner feels safe, seen, and deeply valued.

Donald: Being a man of Masters means; I don't rush love; I build it. I've learned to speak honestly, to show up consistently, and to honour her emotions, not trying to fix or dismiss them. My love isn't just a feeling. It's a decision I make every day. And that decision starts with how I treat myself.

Colleen: Aure Chi is the radiant center of a gentleman's heart, the quiet fire that warms every act of affection. It's the way he gives without keeping score. The way he listens with his whole being. He doesn't cling to outdated roles. He evolves them, offering kindness as a golden gesture, not because he has to, but because it's who he is.

Donald: I hold the door open, not for show, but because I see her. I want her to know she's worth the small things, the thoughtful things. Aure Chi is in the way I touch her back as she enters a room, the way I remember how she likes her coffee, the way I make her feel cherished without saying a word.

Colleen: And then, there's Nobler, the soul of his chivalry. This is where romance becomes sacred. Where ego bows to humility, and loyalty takes the lead. The Nobler doesn't seek to conquer her heart. He seeks to honour it. To protect it. To lift it into a love that's rooted in reverence, not possession.

Donald: Nobler taught me that real strength is in gentleness. True devotion isn't loud; it's steady. It's how I stay when it's hard, how I listen when I don't understand, how I love her not because she completes me but because I choose her every day.

Colleen: In a world where so many men are swept away by the chaos of everyday life, *The "MR" Factor* stands as a reminder: you were made for more. This is more than an image, more than surface gestures. This is about embodying refinement in every room you walk into, especially when no one is watching.

Donald: Becoming a refined man isn't about having it all together. It's about the willingness to grow. To challenge yourself. To show up with integrity when it would be easier to check out. *The "MR" Factor* changed how I see myself, not as someone chasing perfection, but as someone choosing progress.

Colleen: This isn't a checklist of traits. It's a lifestyle. A mindset. A sacred commitment to do better for yourself, your relationships, and the world around you. Chivalry isn't lost. It's reborn through your actions. Through your Master's. Your Aure Chi. Your Nobler.

Donald: I'm not trying to impress anyone anymore. I'm trying to inspire. And the more I grow into this version of myself, the more I attract people, love, and opportunities that reflect the man I've chosen to become. True romance is not a fantasy. It's a reflection of your inner refinement.

Let the Masters guide your discipline. Let Aure Chi soften your soul. Let Nobler lift your love to its highest expression. That's chivalry reborn. That's the modern gentleman. That's *The "MR" Factor.*

INFLUENCE: ORDINARY TO EXTRAORDINARY

The measure of a man is not found in wealth, power, or prestige but in the strength of his character, the depth of his integrity, and the influence he exerts in the lives of others. *The "MR" Factor* is not just a title; it's a transformative force, a commitment to rise above the ordinary and encompass the extraordinary. Its influence extends far beyond personal success; it's a power that shapes the world, leaving an indelible mark on those it touches.

The "MR" Factor is built on values that define a man's presence in society. He is a man of honour, respect, and accountability. While many may associate the term 'gentleman' with chivalry, it is, in fact, more relevant than ever. In a world that often celebrates arrogance and self-interest, the gentleman inspires dignity and purpose, upholding a tradition that transcends time.

At his core, *The "MR" Factor* understands that strength is not measured by dominance but by self-mastery. The gentleman controls his impulses, refines his emotions, and leads with wisdom rather than force. His confidence is not rooted in superiority but in the certainty of his values. He does not demand respect; he earns it through his actions, his words, and the consistency of his principles.

The art of influence is actual influence; it's not forced but cultivated. The gentleman applies influence not through intimidation but through inspiration. His presence demands attention, not because he seeks it, but because he embodies excellence. He listens more than he speaks, values discourse over dictation, and uplifts rather than undermines.

The "MR" Factor recognizes that leadership is not about control, but about empowerment. A gentleman who embodies the *'MR'* does not impose his will; he encourages others to discover their strength. He is a mentor, a role model, and a source of wisdom. He shapes his environment with grace and conviction, whether in business, family, or friendships, empowering those around him to reach their full potential.

The transformation from an ordinary man to an extraordinary gentleman is not about external changes but internal refinement. It begins with self-awareness, an honest assessment of strengths and weaknesses. A gentleman does not fear growth; he welcomes it. He seeks knowledge, hones his skills, and continuously refines his character.

One of the most defining qualities of a gentleman is his ability to adapt without compromising his principles. In every era, there have been men who conform to trends and men who set them. The *'MR'* gentleman is the latter. He does not chase fleeting popularity; he upholds timeless values. In doing so, he becomes an example of strength, an anchor in a shifting world.

The "MR" Factor's influence is most deeply felt in a gentleman's relationships, where his character and actions leave a lasting impact. He understands that respect and kindness are not optional but essential.

He operates with integrity and consideration, whether in personal relationships, friendships, or professional dealings. In romance, he cherishes his partner, seeing her not as a possession but a person of equal worth. His chivalry is genuine, a reflection of his respect for women. He listens, he protects, and most importantly, he nurtures. His love is loyal, and his loyalty is unshakable.

My son, Chance, lived by a quiet code of honour that carried the weight of wisdom beyond his years. He never saw his girlfriends as anything less than his equal, always meeting them with patience, understanding, and unwavering respect.

His presence in their lives wasn't fleeting or superficial; it was deliberate, thoughtful, and deeply felt. He didn't measure his worth by admiration or applause, but by the depth of the connections he built and the lives he gently shaped.

He embodied what it meant to be a gentleman, not in grand gestures or rehearsed chivalry, but in how he was authentic, kind, and wholly present. People gravitated toward him not because he sought their attention but because he made them feel seen, heard, and valued. His influence lingered long after he left the room, a quiet echo of the care he poured into others.

I remember one evening when his girlfriend seemed troubled. Her face carried the weight of something unspoken, her silence louder than words. She shook her head when he asked her what was wrong, insisting it was nothing. For Chance, that was never enough. He stopped everything, gently took her hands, and guided her to sit down. His eyes, filled with quiet determination, met hers, refusing to let her retreat into herself.

"Our relationship will only grow if we're honest with each other," he told her, his voice steady yet tender. "I know something is bothering you. If I've done something to hurt you, I need to know. We must talk about, understand, and make it right."

There was no demand in his words, only an invitation, a safe place where truth could rest without fear. He didn't just listen; he absorbed, reflected, and acted. That was who he was. Not just a young man in love but a man who understood that love was more than words, responsibility, patience, and the willingness to grow together.

Chance didn't just make an impact; he left a lasting impression on everyone who knew him. The kind of impression that sticks with you makes you pause and think about how you show up in the world.

Time moves on, but the way he carried himself, the way he cared, and the way he made people feel all still linger like a melody you can't forget. He didn't just live; he showed others how to live with intention.

Chance had a way of lifting people, of making them feel seen, valued, and understood. His influence wasn't about grand gestures or flashy words; it was in the little things, the moments that mattered, and how he made others feel safe enough to be real. That's the kind of impact that doesn't fade. It spreads like ripples in a pond, reaching far beyond what he could have imagined.

That's the power of *The "MR" Factor*. It's not about arriving at some perfect version of yourself; it's about making a daily choice to be better, lead with integrity, and raise the standard. It's about showing up for people, owning your words, and making sure your actions match them. It takes work and commitment. But in a world full of noise and empty gestures, choosing to be a real gentleman stands out. It makes a difference.

The world needs more men like that, men who don't settle for just "good enough" but who push to be extraordinary. The extraordinary is not reserved for a select few; it is available to any man willing to cultivate his mind, refine his heart, and uplift his soul.

To be a gentleman is to accept this challenge, step into the fullness of one's potential, and employ influence with honour and purpose. And so, to every man who seeks to elevate himself, let this be the call to rise.

That's what *The "MR" Factor* is all about. It's not just an idea; it's a way of life. And the best part? It's a choice any man can make, starting right now. Be the gentleman who transforms the ordinary into the extraordinary. Be the man whose influence changes lives, whose presence inspires, and whose legacy endures. The world is waiting for men of honour. Will you answer the call?

OLIVIA IS MY NAME

Let's have fun before entering *The "MR" Factor* world. I've got a story to tell: three intriguing men, and a captivating woman named Olivia. Here's the question: Which one do you think you are? Who holds *The "MR" Factor*? And most importantly, who does Olivia choose? The answer might surprise you.

Olivia sighed, set her coffee down, and decided she needed a break from the whirlwind of thoughts. Had she decided to meet this guy, Matt, as she stood up and slipped on her coat, her scarf draped loosely around her neck. The crisp morning air greeted her as soon as Olivia stepped outside the café. She inhaled deeply, letting the chill of the air clear her head as she strolled down the street, the hum of the city all around her.

It was here, outside her favourite bookstore, that she first saw Matt. Matt was leaning against a vintage sports car, one hand in his pocket, the other holding a phone to his ear. He gestured as he spoke to someone on the other end, his voice a mix of excitement and charisma. His posture was relaxed, as if he were perfectly at ease in his own skin, as if the world were his stage. His leather jacket fit him like a second skin, and his boots looked like they had seen a few adventures. His sunglasses rested casually on his head, trademarking his effortless coolness.

Olivia smiled to herself. She had always been drawn to that kind of energy, even though she'd never been one to chase after thrills. Matt had this way of lighting up a room or, in his case, a street corner. He wasn't waiting for anything, letting the city move around him while he held everyone's attention. As she walked closer, she heard him laugh, a contagious sound. She raised an eyebrow, almost amused at how he commanded the world's attention.

"You know," she called out, strolling toward him, "if you're going to lean against that car like a movie star, at least make sure the car matches the drama." Matt turned at the sound of her voice, and a grin spread across his face. The kind of grin suggested he knew exactly what he was doing. "Olivia, right?" Matt said, his voice light but carrying an edge of confidence as if their meeting had been written in the stars. He hung up the phone without missing a beat. "I've got to say, you're exactly what I was expecting."

Olivia tilted her head, raising her eyebrow, intrigued despite herself. "And what was that?" He leaned against the car, his posture relaxed, yet still commanding. "Someone unpredictable," he replied smoothly, his eyes twinkling with humour and something else, something challenging. "I could feel it. You've got that energy."

Olivia couldn't help but roll her eyes, crossing her arms. Is that your pickup line? Matt chuckled, a deep, rich sound that made her smile. "Pick-up lines are for amateurs," he said with a shrug, leaning in just a bit closer, his voice lowering slightly. "I like to make things interesting."

Olivia laughed, shaking her head, though the warmth of his presence was undeniable. He had a way of making everything feel spontaneous, as if life were one big game, and he was ready to play. "So, tell me," Matt said, his grin never fading, "what's a woman like you doing on a random Saturday morning?"

Olivia smiled, genuinely intrigued despite being herself. "Just taking a walk, clearing my head." Matt's eyes lit up as if this were the perfect opportunity to sell her on his brand of excitement. "Well, if you need help with that, I've got a few adrenaline-filled ideas. You know, something spontaneous." She shot him a look, the corner of her mouth twitching upward. "I'm good with just the walk, thanks." Matt raised his hands in mock surrender, his grin never faltering. "Alright, alright. But when you're ready for something more exciting, you know where to find me."

Before she could respond, he winked and slipped back into his car, the engine purring to life with a growl as he sped off into the city. Olivia stood there momentarily, shaking her head with a soft chuckle. Matt was the kind of guy who never stopped moving, always in motion, always the life of the party.

He was fun, no doubt, but was that enough? As she continued her walk, she couldn't help but feel that her meeting with Matt had been enjoyable and good. There was an undeniable pull to him, but the question remained: could she find something deeper with a man who seemed to live on the edge?

Olivia stood near the window, her eyes scanning the room with the quiet observation that had become second nature. Unlike many others at this party, she wasn't one to chase the spotlight. The laughter, the clinking of glasses, and the hum of conversation all felt like background noise to her. She preferred to be a quiet observer, watching people interact and analyzing the subtle dynamics. And then, she saw him.

He was standing in the corner, surveying the crowd like a businessman studying a new market. She could feel the energy in the air shift as he surveyed the room. He wasn't just there to mingle but to command the room and ensure everyone knew who he was. Rich was his name, and she already knew enough about him. He was the CEO, the man everyone talked about, who made things happen. He wasn't hard to spot; his presence was like an aura, impossible to ignore.

But it wasn't his wealth or his title that intrigued her. It was something deeper, something she couldn't quite pinpoint yet. There was a sense of control in how he moved, a confidence that didn't seem forced but built into him like it had been there his whole life. Most people might be intimidated by it, but Olivia wasn't. If anything, it made her curious. It was a challenge she wasn't sure she was ready to face but couldn't help but want to. And then, as if the universe had decided to send him her way,

Rich started walking toward her. It wasn't just a casual stroll but measured and purposeful, like he was preparing to close a deal. She could almost see the gears turning in his head, and that made her smile to herself. She wasn't one to be impressed by titles, but it seemed like this man was used to impressing others. She couldn't help but wonder how he'd approach her.

When he finally reached her, he greeted her with the same confident smile she had seen from across the room, but there was something in his eyes, a flicker of curiosity. It was like he had something to prove but wasn't sure what. Maybe he was just like the others, trying to impress her with his resume and status, or maybe there was more to him than that.

"I've always believed that people are a lot like investments," he said, his voice smooth, almost like he delivered a well-rehearsed pitch. "You have to know when to commit, when to diversify, and when to take risks." She raised an eyebrow, unsure if he was trying to impress her or make some grand statement. But she wasn't going to make it easy for him. After all, she had heard her fair share of sales pitches and wasn't looking for another one. "Are you telling me that love is like a stock portfolio?" she asked, her tone playful but skeptical.

Rich chuckled. It wasn't a forced laugh; there was a genuine warmth, making her reconsider the walls she had built around herself. He wasn't acting like the typical guy who would throw out clever lines to win her over. He was trying to connect with her in his way, and for some reason, she respected that. "Not exactly," he said, shaking his head slightly, his smile still in place. "But if you're willing to put in the time and energy, you can get returns worth more than any number on a balance sheet." Her lips curled into a smile.

There it was again, how Rich didn't just say words but somehow made them feel real. He wasn't discussing stock options or major corporate deals. No, he was talking about something deeper, something she couldn't entirely ignore. She laughed softly, more out of appreciation than anything else.

"I'll take that as a compliment, Mr. CEO," she said, her voice carrying a hint of amusement. And that was when she felt it. That slight shift occurred when the conversation moved from the abstract to something personal.

She wasn't just talking to a guy with a fancy title anymore; she was talking to a man who seemed interested in something more than himself. Olivia could tell Rich had spent most of his life building an empire. But what surprised her wasn't the empire itself but the vulnerability she felt creeping into their conversation.

He wasn't just talking about business anymore. He spoke about taking risks, making connections, and allowing himself to be open in a way that most people with his status wouldn't dare to. And for someone like Olivia, who had always prided herself on being observant and honest, that made her take notice.

There was something about the way Rich carried himself, the way he interacted with her, that made her reconsider her usual approach to men. Most guys came with an agenda, a script they followed, but not Rich. No, he wasn't trying to impress her with his wealth or position. He wasn't talking about his latest acquisition or the next big deal. He was talking about life, about risk, about what mattered.

And Olivia? Well, she wasn't used to this. It was like a breath of fresh air. The depth of the conversation and the genuine interest in what she had to say made her feel like she wasn't just another person in the crowd. It made her feel like she was being seen for who she was, not what people assumed she was.

For the first time in a long time, Olivia felt herself being pulled into someone's world. She wasn't sure what it meant yet or where it might go, but she couldn't deny the connection that was forming between them. Rich's sincerity was rare in her world of surface-level interactions. And though she wasn't one to jump to conclusions, she knew one thing for sure: she wanted to know more.

The soft hum of the city was punctuated by the gentle ringing of church bells in the distance as Olivia walked through the park. It was late afternoon, and the light began softening, casting a golden hue over the trees and grass. The moment was peaceful; it was exactly what she needed: time to think and breathe.

She wasn't looking for anything when she turned a corner near the fountain. But then, she saw him. Julian. He stood by a small, secluded bench, focused on a book he was reading, completely absorbed in it. He wasn't dressed for a business meeting or a night out but in elegant yet straightforward attire: dark jeans, a soft sweater, and a trench coat that fit him perfectly. There was no rush in his demeanour, no need to impress, just a man fully engaged in his world.

Olivia hesitated for a moment, unsure if she should interrupt. But something about his stillness drew her in. There was serenity in his presence that she hadn't seen in either Matt or Rich, who always seemed to have an agenda. On the other hand, Julian appeared to exist just for the moment's sake. She walked closer, her footsteps quiet on the grass.

As she approached, she noticed the book in his hands; it was a rare poetry collection by Rainer Maria Rilke, an author Olivia had always admired. Without looking up from the pages, Julian spoke calmly, almost knowing, "Olivia, if you're looking to steal my copy, I should warn you, it's my favourite edition." She stopped, surprised. "You knew I was coming?" He glanced up, the corners of his mouth turning up in a soft, amused smile. "Not really. But I had a feeling. You're the type of person who is always searching for the next layer beneath the surface.

I can sense it. She raised an eyebrow, amused. "You're quite the observer, aren't you?" "I try to be," he replied, closing the book gently. "Sometimes, it's in the stillness that we understand the most. In the quiet, we find what's been hiding." Olivia looked at him for a long moment, intrigued. "You believe that?"

"I do," Julian said, his voice steady and thoughtful. "Not just about others, but about ourselves, too. We spend so much time moving, rushing, and looking for answers outside of ourselves.

But sometimes, the answers are right here. All we need is a moment of quiet." She couldn't help but smile, feeling a sense of comfort that she hadn't expected. "You're a bit of an idealist, aren't you?" He shrugged; his expression was thoughtful but not defensive. "I wouldn't call it idealism. I'd say it's more of an appreciation for what's real, the things that matter. The moments that connect us to the world without noise."

Olivia couldn't help but be drawn to him. There was no bravado, no need to impress. He had a quiet confidence in being exactly who he was. "I think I could use a little more of that," she admitted, her voice softer than expected. Julian set the book down on the bench and looked up at her, his gaze steady. "Maybe that's why we're here. Remind each other that it's okay to step back and be."

She sat on the bench beside him, not knowing what she was doing but feeling at peace in a way she hadn't in a long time. The city felt miles away, the park enveloping them in its tranquility. After a few moments of comfortable silence, Olivia turned to him, her curiosity piqued. "So, how did you come to appreciate these quiet moments? The ones that others might miss?"

Julian hesitated, his eyes flicking over the horizon before meeting hers. "I think life teaches you to appreciate stillness when you've been through enough noise," he said quietly as if the words had weight. "I learned to find peace in the chaos by stepping away from it. It's been a journey that taught me more about myself than anything else." Olivia studied him, sensing more behind his words, but she didn't push. Instead, she let the moment settle between them, the unspoken understanding of shared space and presence weaving its way into the conversation.

A breeze rustled the leaves, and Donald smiled softly. "Sometimes, it's not about talking, Olivia. Sometimes, it's about being. "She nodded slowly, feeling something shift inside her. There was something about the simplicity of his words, the way he allowed silence to speak volumes. At that moment, she felt like she could understand him in a way she hadn't with the others. Matt and Rich had their strengths but felt like they were always trying to impress or win.

But Julian? He was present. As the sun began to dip lower in the sky, Olivia stood up, stretching her arms above her head. "I should be going," she said, her voice light but thoughtful. Julian stood as well, his gaze steady. "It's rare. Sometimes, the best connections don't require words or grand gestures. They require us to show up." Olivia looked at him, her heart stirring. "I think I understand that now."

Before she turned to leave, Julian placed a hand on the back of the bench, his voice low and sincere. "I'm glad you stopped by, Olivia. I think we can both learn a great deal from these moments. But it's not always about learning, you know. Sometimes, it's about allowing things to unfold." With a final, soft smile, Olivia turned and walked away, but this time, she didn't feel as uncertain.

There were still Matt and Rich, but Julian had left a lasting impression in her mind's quiet spaces. As she walked through the park and out into the bustling city, she couldn't shake the feeling that life was beginning to show her something she had yet to understand fully. The mystery of it all, of who would truly captivate her, still lingered. The question remained, though: Could one man, one moment, change everything? And it was a mystery worth pursuing.

THE STORY OF NOAH

This is the story of the *M*an of *R*efinement, crafted to give you, the reader, a deeper understanding of how and why this plays a pivotal role in *The "MR" Factor*. So, there's this man, let's call him Noah, who thought love was supposed to be like the perfect story. He was on a quest to uncover the ultimate narrative that would reveal the magic of true romance.

Noah was a bit of a dreamer. In his mind, love was a story with all the drama, adventure, and heart-wrenching moments he'd read about in novels. He thought that finding that perfect tale would be the key to unlocking everything he ever wanted in love; a love that was just right. And maybe he could find his way to that happily ever after.

One sunny afternoon, Noah found himself wandering through a busy marketplace. The hustle and bustle of vendors selling fruits, spices, and trinkets filled the air. People moved quickly, exchanging coins, chatting with each other, and going about their daily business. But amidst all this, something caught his attention. Over to the side, near a little corner by a vendor with brightly coloured scarves, sat a young woman. She wasn't selling anything, but her presence was magnetic.

She was a storyteller known throughout the marketplace for telling tales that made you laugh, cry, and everything. The way she spoke had a certain magic; her words were like plots that tugged at your heart and made you believe in the power of love, even if you hadn't felt it in years. Her stories weren't just stories; they were an experience. They said her words had a kind of magic that made you feel everything: the joy, the heartbreak, the hope, all at once.

Curiosity got the best of Noah. He was always a seeker, always looking for answers, especially about love. So, he approached the storyteller, his heart full of questions, and asked, "How do you tell such incredible stories? How do you make people feel so much with just your words?"

The young woman looked up at him, her eyes twinkling with that knowing smile only someone who had lived through enough to understand life's messy beauty could wear. She was the guide Noah didn't know he needed. "Well, Noah," she said, "love is just like a story. It's not about having the perfect beginning and not wrapping everything up in a neat little bow at the end. No, it's all about the chapters in between: the twists, the turns, the highs, and the lows. You can't rush it. You can't force it. You have to live it, one page at a time."

Noah stood there, taking in her words. He'd never thought of love that way, so raw and unpredictable. But how she said it made him feel like he had just been handed a key to something he had been searching for. Her words were like a beacon of hope, illuminating his new path. She reached into a small bag beside her and pulled out a blank book and a pen. "Here," she said, handing them to him. "Start writing. But don't try to write the perfect love story. Just write your heart."

Noah took the book, its pages crisp and white, and stared at the pen. For a moment, he felt unsure. What did he have to write? What if he couldn't get it right? But the storyteller's calm voice echoed in his mind: Write your heart. So, he sat down right there in the market and started. The first chapter he wrote was full of fire, intense passion, excitement, and chemistry that made your heart race, and your palms sweat. The second chapter? Well, it wasn't as smooth. There were misunderstandings, awkward silences, and moments of confusion where neither person knew what to do. But Noah didn't stop. He just kept writing, letting the story unfold.

He began to realize that love wasn't about everything being flawless. The messier parts, the parts that felt rough around the edges, were the moments that made the characters real. They weren't just two perfect people in an ideal world. They were learning, growing, stumbling, and laughing together. And that, in its way, was a beautiful love story.

As the pages filled up, Noah wrote about the little moments of connection, the ones where two people didn't need words to understand each other. He wrote about compromise, about how love wasn't about always getting what you wanted but about giving and taking in a way that made both people feel seen and valued. He wrote about forgiveness, those challenging moments when things went wrong, but they worked through the storm and came out stronger on the other side. And then there were the chapters filled with laughter, the kind of laughter that made your stomach-ache and your eyes water, where everything felt so right that you couldn't help but savour every moment.

Noah wasn't just writing about a love story anymore; he was writing about his love story, about how it unfolded in real-time. With every page and word, he realized something that shifted his perspective: love isn't about perfecting everything. It's about showing up for each other, embracing the unexpected, and walking through life's challenges hand in hand. Even when the road wasn't smooth, those moments mattered most. This was not just a love story, but a journey of self-discovery and personal growth.

He wrote about the quiet moments of connection, when two people didn't need words to understand one another. He wrote about compromise, where love wasn't just about winning but finding a middle ground. And, of course, he wrote about forgiveness when things got tough, but love found a way to heal. But there were also the chapters of joy, laughter-filled pages where they couldn't stop teasing each other, where humour became a glue that kept them together. Those chapters, too, were just as crucial as the heart-to-heart moments. They were the ones who filled their love story with light and laughter, making it a joyous journey.

When he finally put the pen down, Noah looked away from the pages, feeling a sense of peace, he hadn't expected. The storyteller was still sitting there, watching him with a gentle smile on her face. "I think I get it now," he said, the weight of his realization settling in. "Romance isn't about having the perfect love story. It's about writing your story together, wherever it leads you." The storyteller's advice echoed in his mind, reminding him that love is not about perfection but the journey and experiences.

The storyteller's smile deepened as if she knew the lesson had sunk in. "Exactly," she said, her voice filled with warmth. The awkward, beautiful, unpredictable parts of love make it worth living, the chapters you didn't see coming, the ones that change you. It's about the love you build between. That's what makes the story yours."

Noah stood up, feeling a quiet confidence; a sense of peace settled into his heart. He walked away from the marketplace full of his thoughts and feelings, a new understanding of love burning brightly in his heart. Love wasn't something to search for; it was something to create, to live, and to write with the person who walks beside you, one chapter at a time. The perfect love story wasn't about finding the right words but about living the right story. Together.

OLD-STYLE WITH MODERN EXPECTATIONS

Colleen: Navigating the balance between tradition and modern life isn't always easy, is it? We're living in a time when old-school values and modern trends are constantly at odds. One moment, you want to handwrite a note. The next, you're texting because it's quicker. However, I still believe in the power of traditional gestures, such as a sincere hug, a home-cooked meal, or a genuine "thank you."

Donald: Absolutely. The world moves fast, but there's something timeless about those small, thoughtful things. A handwritten note might seem outdated, but it carries weight, a message that says, "I took the time for you." And let's not forget how grounding it feels when someone looks you in the eye with intent instead of just sending an emoji.

Colleen: Exactly. It's not about resisting the modern world but asking: how do we keep the heart in it all? For instance, remember when a handshake meant everything? It was trust in your palm, a simple, silent contract of respect.

Donald: And now, it's a wave on a screen or an air high-five. But the meaning doesn't have to vanish. Eye contact, posture, and even tone those subtle cues still carry the message of dignity and regard. It's not the gesture itself that matters most. It's the intention behind it.

Colleen: Now, let's talk gift-giving. I've always believed in thoughtful gifts, something personal, something chosen with care. But today, it's tempting to hit "add to cart" and call it a day.

Donald: True, but even digital gifts can carry depth if we layer in meaning. A gift card paired with a handwritten note. A package with a surprise detail. It's not about going backward. It's about going deeper. That's what keeps giving beautiful.

Colleen: Communication is where we see the most significant clash. I still love a good phone call or handwritten card. They slow us down and make us feel seen. But everyone's used to instant everything now.

Donald: And yet, when you pick up the phone instead of sending a quick text, it hits differently. It shows presence. It says, "You're worth my time." If we scheduled even a single in-depth conversation each week, our relationships would feel more alive and more anchored.

Colleen: Let's not forget the dinner table. Meals used to be our sacred space where stories were shared, lessons learned, and laughter filled the room. These days, we're lucky if we're not multitasking through lunch.

Donald: That's one tradition I'll always defend. A dinner table isn't just a surface. It's a sanctuary. It's where kids hear family history in recipe form and learn respect without a lecture. That kind of tradition shapes people. It builds character.

Colleen: Family dinners taught me that love shows up in simple ways. The clatter of dishes, the passing of bread, the moment when someone says, "Tell me about your day." That's legacy.

Donald: Legacy lives in the pauses, those moments we stop to care, to show up, to honour each other. In a world racing forward, tradition is our anchor.

Colleen: And modernity is our sail. We don't need to choose one over the other. We blend them. We honour handwritten notes and still send texts saying, "thinking of you." We host dinners and still enjoy a virtual coffee date. It's all about intentional harmony.

Donald: It's about showing up with meaning, whether that's through a screen or a hug. You don't have to abandon tradition to evolve. You carry it forward with grace and relevance.

Colleen: So, here's to both the handshake and the nod, the note and the text, the home-cooked meal and the convenience click. We don't have to choose sides. We need to choose intention.

Donald: Exactly. Because when tradition and modern life walk hand in hand, that's where real connection lives.

MASTERING THE ART OF COMMUNICATION

Colleen: Imagine us, yes, you and me, sitting down for a conversation. No fluff, no formalities, just real talk about something that shapes every part of our lives: communication. Not just talking, not just hearing, but truly connecting.

If communication were only about words, the loudest voices would always win. But we both know that's not the case. You've seen someone walk into a room, and without saying a word, they command attention. Or maybe you've met someone who makes you feel like the only person in the world just by how they listen. That's communication. That's the art of it.

I've spent a lifetime observing, learning, and refining my approach to connecting with others. And if there's one thing I know for sure, it's this: the best communicators aren't the best talkers; they're the best listeners. I won't lie; I love talking as much as listening. Why? When I speak, my goal is to share something meaningful, and when I listen, I gain something valuable in return.

I remember sitting on my patio with a dear friend as she shared stories of her ventures, the ones that brought her joy and the ones that carried sorrow. I listened as she spoke, offering my thoughts only when she asked. When it was time for her to leave, we hugged, and she looked into my eyes with a gentle smile, thanking me for listening. I smiled back and said, "Anytime."

Then she said something that stayed with me: "Colleen, you listened, not just to my words, but to what I felt. You were truly interested and did it with such kindness when you shared your thoughts." I thanked her, touched by her words. And then she added, "People like you are rare. If more of us had your gift, the world would be a much happier."

Her gratitude warmed my heart, not because of the compliment but because I had been able to give her a space where she felt heard, understood, and valued. And really, isn't that what we all need? A reminder that our words and our feelings matter.

Have you ever been in a conversation where the other person was obviously waiting for their turn to speak? Frustrating, right? I've encountered this more times than I can count, and when I sense that kind of listener, I don't hesitate to cut the conversation short. Why waste time? But real listening, the kind where someone truly absorbs, processes, and responds with intention; that's where the magic happens.

Donald: Communication isn't just about the words you choose; it's about how you say them. Try saying, "That's interesting" in different tones: curious, sarcastic, bored, surprised- exact words, but with entirely different meanings. And in today's world of texts, emails, and social media, tone gets lost all the time and ever had a message completely misinterpreted? That's why a simple "okay" can feel cold, while an "okay" with an emoji showing your emotion can change the entire vibe.

Colleen: Then there's confidence. Have you ever noticed how people believe what you say when you believe what you say? Confidence isn't about being the loudest in the room; it's about owning your words. Whether you're making a point, telling a story, or simply introducing yourself, confidence turns words into impact. But let's be clear: Confidence isn't arrogance. Arrogance repels; confidence attracts. The difference? A confident person invites conversation, listens as much as they speak, and stands gracefully.

Donald: But words alone won't do the job. Your body is speaking even when you're silent. Crossed arms can make you seem closed off, slouching can signal disinterest, and avoiding eye contact can weaken your message before you even say a word. On the other hand, standing tall, making eye contact, and using purposeful gestures? That's a silent language that commands attention and respect.

And here's a question: do you talk to your boss like you do to your best friend? Hopefully not. Great communicators adapt. I read the room, adjust my energy, and tailor my message without losing authenticity. This isn't about being fake, it's about being effective.

Colleen: But if there's one thing I want you to take away from this, it's that people remember stories, not facts. You can throw statistics at someone all day, but they'll feel it if you tell them a story. And when people feel something, they remember it. That's why the most outstanding leaders, speakers, and even comedians use storytelling as their secret weapon.

Communication isn't just a skill; it's an art that takes a lifetime to refine. The more we practice listening, adjusting our tone, using confident body language, and telling compelling stories, the more our words matter. So, whether you're trying to inspire, persuade, connect, or be understood, remember this: communication is more than words. It's connection. Its influence. It's power. And like any great art, it takes practice.

Donald: Alright, let's get to it. We want to teach you not just the idea of listening and speaking thoughtfully, but how to do it. These aren't just skills for the fancy boardroom or a special event; they're for everyday life with friends, family, and yourself. When you learn to use them effectively, your relationships grow stronger and begin to command more respect and trust. Here's how you do it.

Lesson 1: Mastering the Power of Listening

Listening isn't just about hearing words; it's about understanding. Here's how to do it in a way that will make people feel truly seen and heard.

Step 1: Be Present
This may sound simple, but it's more complicated than you think. It means entirely focusing on the person in front of you. When listening, put down the phone, step away from distractions, and make eye contact. Your attention is a precious gift; use it wisely.

Example: If someone shares their day with you, don't let your mind wander to your thoughts or problems. Instead, lean in a little, nod occasionally to show you're with them, and keep your mind focused on their words.

Step 2: Don't Interrupt
Here's a big one. I've learned that the best listeners resist the urge to jump in with their thoughts or advice. Let the other person speak fully. If you interrupt, you're not truly listening; you're waiting for your turn to talk.

Example: If a friend is venting about work, don't jump in immediately with solutions. Instead, let them finish and ask, "What do you think you'll do next?" or "How are you feeling about that?"

Step 3: Reflect Back What You Hear
A great way to show that you're listening is to reflect on what the person said by paraphrasing or asking follow-up questions. It lets them know you're taking it all in and helps clarify any misunderstandings.

Example: "It sounds like you're frustrated about your meeting today. Do you want to talk more about what happened?"

Lesson 2: The Art of Thoughtful Speaking

Now, let's explore the power of speaking thoughtfully. Your words have the potential to shape understanding, build relationships, and make a lasting impact. Understanding how to use them effectively can ensure that your words work for you, not against you, in every interaction.

Step 1: Pause Before Speaking
I can't stress this enough. Thoughtful speaking starts with a moment of pause. Before you speak, take a beat to think: What am I trying to say? Why am I saying it? How will it land on the other person? This moment of reflection ensures your words have the right tone and intent.

Example: When a colleague asks you for feedback, pause for a second instead of immediately blurting out what's on your mind. Think about what will be most helpful. Instead of just saying, "I didn't like your report," you could say, "I think the structure of your report is solid. Maybe we could work on making the main points a little clearer?"

Step 2: Be Clear and Concise
Over-explaining or rambling clouds the point you're trying to make. Thoughtful speaking is about being transparent and precise with your words. Don't overcomplicate things.

Example: If you need to express an opinion, don't bury it under a mountain of qualifiers. Instead of saying, "I kind of think, maybe, possibly, it would be a good idea if we could...," say, "I think it would be best if we could try."

Step 3: Consider the Other Person's Feelings
Empathy is the cornerstone of effective communication. When you consider how your words will affect the other person, you can choose a tone and approach that uplifts rather than puts down. This is especially important in sensitive situations.

Example: If someone has done something wrong, instead of saying, "You messed up big time," you could say, "I think there's a way we can approach this to improve next time. Let's figure it out together."

Lesson 3: Finding the Balance Between Listening and Speaking

The key to building strong relationships is knowing when to listen and when to speak. It's a delicate balance, and you'll get better at it the more you practice.

Step 1: Assess the Situation
If the person opens up or the conversation is emotionally charged, it's time to listen. If the person asks for your thoughts or advice, that's your cue to speak thoughtfully.

Example: If a friend is sharing something personal, let them talk. If they ask, "What do you think I should do?" it's time for you to weigh in but do so with kindness.

Step 2: Use the "Wait and See" Approach
Before sharing your thoughts, take a moment. Sometimes, the best thing you can do is wait and see if the other person needs more space to share. Don't rush to fix or fill the silence.

Example: If your partner is upset, don't rush in with "It'll be okay" or "Here's what you need to do." Instead, give them time to say what's really on their mind.

Step 3: Adjust Based on Feedback
Pay attention to the other person's responses, whether verbal or nonverbal. If they seem like they need more listening, keep it going. If they're waiting for you to speak, it's time to step up with your thoughtful words.

Example: If you notice your friend nodding and looking relieved as you listen, it's a good sign that they just needed someone to hear them. If they look confused or uncertain, that's your cue to gently guide the conversation forward with your insight.

Alright, gentlemen, here's one more thing to consider regarding communication. If your woman is upset, take a moment to listen with no thoughtful feedback. Speaking from experience, I'll tell you, there's nothing more frustrating than being upset and having my partner plunge straight into giving me advice when all I wanted was for him to pull me close, say, "Everything's going to be okay," and remind me that he's there for me. Sometimes, it's not about fixing the problem; it's about offering comfort.

Listening and speaking thoughtfully are skills that take time to master. It's about being aware of when it's your time to listen and when it's your time to share. Practice these steps and use them in real-life situations; you'll soon notice stronger connections and more respect in your relationships. Be patient with yourself but also take action. The world needs more people who know how to listen and speak purposefully. You're well on your way to becoming one of them.

Body language and its impact on perception
My journey into understanding body language began on stage. While words are important, the audience craves more. They need movement, expressions, and tone; without these, they might miss the essence or lose interest. As time passed, I found myself enrolling in courses on body language. That's when everything fell into place. It was a transformative journey for me, those I care about, and everyone I interact with. It's like a secret language that unites us all, enhancing our communication and connection.

Let's take a crash course on body language that can transform your daily communication. You might not always realize it, but sometimes, how you carry yourself, stand, sit, and even move your hands says a lot more than words. And guess what? The same goes for the way you read someone else's body language. Trust me, mastering this will help you connect with people in ways you can't imagine. Let me walk you through it.

Lesson 1: Understanding Your Body Language
Before deciphering the body language of others, it is crucial to be in tune with your own. How are you presenting yourself? Is your posture closed off, or are you open and inviting? Are you standing tall or slouching? Understanding these aspects of your body language is the first step towards effective communication.

Here's the deal: if you want to come across as confident, approachable, and engaged, your body language must match that. Good posture is key. Stand up straight, with your shoulders back. Don't be stiff but give off a comfortable vibe in your skin. This simple adjustment can instantly make you appear more confident and approachable.

Example: The next time you walk into a room, try entering with your chest open, your head held high, and making eye contact with a friendly smile. See how people respond. It's like an unspoken invitation for them to engage with you.

But it's not just about your stance. Pay attention to your gestures, too. Crossing your arms, for example, can signal that you're closed off or defensive, even if you don't mean it. Instead, try keeping your hands relaxed at your side or using open gestures when you talk. It shows that you're open, friendly, and ready to connect.

Lesson 2: Reading Other People's Body Language
Now, let's discuss reading other people's body language. It's not just about decoding their non-verbal cues but also about understanding their unspoken feelings. Their posture, facial expressions, and even their movements can reveal a great deal about their emotional state. This understanding can help you be more empathetic and considerate in your interactions.

For example, if someone is avoiding eye contact, crossing their arms, or leaning away from you, it might be a sign that they're uncomfortable or not fully engaged. But if they're leaning in, maintaining eye contact, and nodding along as you speak, they're likely interested in what you have to say.

Example: Imagine you're conversing with someone, and they're constantly looking at their phone or shifting around in their seat. It's a good sign they're distracted or not fully present. You'll know they're not really with you at that moment.

One thing to watch for is mirroring. If you're speaking to someone and they start to mimic your gestures, posture, or expressions, that's usually a good sign that they feel comfortable and connected with you. It's a natural, subconscious way of saying, "Hey, I'm on the same page as you."

Lesson 3: Body Language in Emotional Situations
Alright, here's where it gets exciting. When emotions are involved, body language becomes even more powerful. If someone's upset, angry, or anxious, you can often pick up on it before they say a word. They might clench their fists, tap their foot, or tighten their jaws. Recognizing these signs allows you to step in and give them space or offer comfort. This preparedness can make you a more supportive presence in their lives.

Let's go back to the example of when your partner is upset. If she's talking about something bothering her, but she's got her arms crossed, is looking down, or is fidgeting, it might mean she's feeling defensive or closed off. That's your cue to adjust your approach to her. Maybe give her some space to breathe or offer a gentle, "Hey, I'm here for you," while ensuring your body language stays open and inviting.

Example: If you notice your partner is closed off, don't immediately bombard her with questions or advice. Instead, soften your tone, give her some space, and show with your body language that you're there to support her, not judge or fix her problem.

Lesson 4: The Power of the Subtle
Small gestures can carry significant weight in communication. A simple touch on the shoulder, a gentle nod, or a smile can speak volumes in a conversation. These subtle body language cues can bridge the gap and convey empathy and understanding when words fail to do so.

Example: Think about the time someone hugged you when you needed it. They didn't say anything, but just being there and offering comfort meant more than words ever could. That's the power of body language in action.

Your body language is just as important, if not more important, than what comes out of your mouth. How you present yourself, how you respond to others, and how you read the room all contribute to how you're perceived. So, start paying attention to your posture, gestures, and facial expressions. When you can connect with others non-verbally, you'll find that your relationships deepen, your communication strengthens, and you start getting a lot more out of every conversation.

Remember, effective communication is not just about what you say or how you make people feel with your presence. The more mindful you are of your body language, the more you'll be able to connect on a deeper, more authentic level. So, pay attention to your posture, gestures, and facial expressions. When you can connect with others non-verbally, you'll find that your relationships deepen, and your communication strengthens.

The art of debate and disagreement with class & importance

Let's talk about two essential skills that can set you apart: the art of debate and disagreement with class, and the importance of a firm handshake and direct eye contact. These little things have a significant impact on how you're perceived and how you connect with people. Stick with me, and I'll show you how mastering these can boost your confidence and relationships in ways you might not have expected.

My Mom and I used to debate about all sorts of things. Sometimes, we'd agree; other times, we wouldn't. But one thing was sure: we both loved to have our say. We were both opinionated; honestly, there's nothing wrong with that.

At least you've got an opinion. Our debates were not just about expressing our views, but also about understanding each other's perspectives. The amusing thing is that the outcome of some of our debates was agreeing to disagree. And then, we'd high-five and laugh it off. No hard feelings, just different views.

When it comes to handshakes, I've got tiny hands, tiny but graceful, if I do say so myself. So, I used to give this gentle handshake, soft but still with direct eye contact. For some reason, I've always felt a need to look into people's eyes and see what's there, as if I could sense something about their feelings. This fascination with eye contact stems from an old saying my uncle used to talk about: "The eyes are the window to the soul." He meant that a person's eyes can reveal their true feelings and thoughts, and those words stuck with me.

One day, I met a business associate who left a lasting impression. As we shook hands, he imparted advice that has since become a guiding principle in my life. He said, "Your handshake is the first impression you give someone. It tells them who you are." He looked at my tiny hands and said, "Those tiny hands of yours should give the most powerful handshake you can because that's who you are."

This advice sparked a transformation in me. Now, when I shake someone's hand, I aim to convey the strength of my spirit, even in this small package. It's my way of showing them, "I might be small, but I've got a lot of heart."

Lesson 1: The Art of Debate and Disagreement with Class
Here's the deal: We all disagree from time to time. It's human nature. But how do you handle those disagreements? That's

what sets you apart. If you want to be someone who leaves a positive impression, even when things get heated, you've got to learn the art of debating with class.

First, it's all about respect. Even if you feel strongly about your point, you lose the conversation the second you start talking down to someone or dismissing their view. Instead, focus on the ideas, not the person. Focus on what's being said, not how it's being said.

Example: If you're in a heated debate, don't raise your voice, don't roll your eyes, don't interrupt. Instead, take a deep breath, stay calm, and listen to the other person's words before responding. Acknowledge their point of view first, then share yours. "I see where you're coming from, but here's how I see it…" is much more powerful than "You're wrong, and here's why."

You don't have to win every argument. Sometimes the best thing to do is agree to disagree and let the other person know you respect their opinion, even if you don't share it. That's how you maintain class and dignity, no matter the topic.

Lesson 2: The Importance of a Firm Handshake and Direct Eye Contact

Now, let's talk about your first impression when meeting someone. We've all been in that situation where you shake someone's hand and it's either too limp or too strong. Both are awkward, and neither says "I've got confidence." A firm handshake, neither too soft nor too hard, is the key. It shows that you're confident without being overbearing. It's a simple move that goes a long way.

Example: The next time you introduce yourself, extend your hand confidently, look the other person in the eye, and offer a handshake that's strong enough to show you mean business, but not so hard that you crush their hand. That balance indicates that you're approachable but also confident.

Then there's eye contact. This one's huge. When you're talking to someone or shaking their hand, look them in the eye. It shows that you're present, engaged, and respectful. It's like saying, "I see you, I hear you, and I value this moment with you." But don't go overboard. Holding eye contact for too long can be uncomfortable, so find that sweet spot where you're making a connection without staring them down.

Example: Avoid looking around the room or glancing at your phone when shaking hands and maintaining eye contact. Keep focus on the person in front of you. This builds trust and conveys a sense that says, "I'm here with you."

Lesson 3: Combining It All
Now, if you want to master the art of class and confidence, here's the secret sauce: Combine the skills of debating with respect, a firm handshake, and direct eye contact. This combo will take your personal and professional relationships to the next level.

When you disagree with someone, do it respectfully, but also own it with a confident posture and steady eye contact. And when you meet someone new, nail that handshake and look them in the eye so they can tell you're someone who knows how to carry themselves with class.

Remember, it's all about balance. You want to show you're confident but not arrogant, respectful but not passive. A firm handshake, calm debates, and steady eye contact convey that you know who you are and are ready to engage with others powerfully and respectfully.

CHIVALRY ISN'T DEAD – IT JUST GREW UP

Colleen: Alright, gentlemen. Let's have an honest talk. You've heard it: "Chivalry is dead." Some even blame feminism for it. But let's get something straight: feminism didn't kill chivalry. At its core, feminism is about equality. And modern chivalry? It prospers on that same principle. It's not about power plays or outdated roles. It's about respect, kindness, and class.

It's about showing up as your best self and treating others, yes, especially women, the way you'd want someone to treat your mother, your sister, or even you when life hits hard. That gentlemen, is the Aure Chi Pillar: leading with heart, emotional intelligence, and presence.

Donald: Now, before anyone rolls their eyes, let's clarify, this isn't about being a knight in shining armour. It's about being a man in control of his presence. Chivalry today isn't a performance. It's a principle. A man who lives with dignity doesn't need applause. That's Nobler conduct: you do it not to be seen but because it's who you are. And let's be clear: modern chivalry doesn't rely on dramatic gestures. No need to toss your coat into a puddle. What matters? The quiet acts that reveal character.

Colleen: So, let's get practical. Holding the door open? It's simple. If you're first to the door, hold it. It doesn't matter who's behind you: woman, man, grandma, delivery guy. This one small move blends the Aure Chi empathy, the Nobler grace, and the Masters daily discipline.

Donald: Next, walking on the outside of the sidewalk. It's about being aware. You're not playing a hero. You're just tuned in. That's the Masters Pillar at work. Quiet protectiveness. Not for performance, for presence.

Colleen: Pulling out a chair? That's subtle Nobler refinement. Offering your coat? That's Aure Chi compassion. Just notice. If she's cold, hand her your jacket; no speech is needed. It's the quiet grace that speaks loudest. And checking in after she gets home? That's not clingy. That's care. With its emotional presence and masculine steadiness, Aure Chi meets the Masters.

Donald: Listening truly listening is chivalry's most underrated power move. Not just nodding while your mind drifts. I mean, active listening. That's all three pillars locked in: Masters: being present. Aure Chi: connecting emotionally. Nobler: honouring someone's voice.

Colleen: And when it comes to paying the bill, offer. If she insists, let her. If she appreciates the gesture, own it. Confidence doesn't dominate. It adapts. That's Nobler respect with Aure Chi grace.

Donald: Every action means more when it flows from the right foundation. That's why we built *The "MR" Factor* on three core pillars: Masters Pillar: Presence, responsibility, and strength in action. Aure Chi Pillar: Kindness, emotional intelligence, and compassion. Nobler Pillar: Refinement, dignity, and elevated behaviour.

Colleen: Modern chivalry isn't extinct. It's evolving. And right now, it needs men who are willing to rise into it.

Donald: Now, for the gentlemen aiming higher, some bonus moves: Stand when she enters the room. Please don't overdo it. Just rise. Acknowledge. Return. Let her order first. It's not theatre. It's simple awareness. And for heaven's sake, put the phone away. Nothing kills presence faster than scrolling while she's talking.

Colleen: Modern chivalry is about being a decent human being with a touch of extra style. It's about noticing. It's about caring. It's about making people feel valued, especially the women in your life. Because at the heart of all this, chivalry isn't a rulebook. It's a rhythm. A standard. A signal of respect.

Donald: And that respect? It's a two-way street. Mutual. Strong. Lasting. Chivalry isn't about impressing the world. It's about honouring your own code. So go on hold the door. Walk the right side of the sidewalk. Offer your coat. And for the love of everything noble, listen. That's how modern gentlemen move.

When mastering the art of genuine courtesy:
To be condescending or not to be; that is the question. I aim to equip you with the knowledge and skills to communicate respectfully without coming across as condescending.

Let's discuss something we've all experienced: trying to be respectful but inadvertently coming across as condescending. It happens to the best of us. You think you're polite, helpful, maybe even a little wise, and suddenly, you get "the look" from the other person. You know, the one, the tight-lipped smile, the raised eyebrow, the subtle shift that screams, Did you talk to me like I'm five?

So, how do you stay respectful without making people feel like you're talking down to them? Let's explore this question.

1. Respect is About Tone, Not Just Words
You can say the same sentence in two different ways, and one will sound kind while the other drips with condescension.

Example:
Respectful: "Oh, I didn't know that! Thanks for explaining."

Condescending: "Ohhh, I seeee so that's what you meant." (Cue the slow nod and smirk.) See the difference? The words alone aren't the problem. It's the tone, the facial expressions, and even the pauses that can make or break a conversation.

Quick Fix:
Be genuine in your tone. If you're thanking someone, mean it. If you're surprised, don't exaggerate it like they discovered fire.

2. Don't Assume People Don't Know Things
Nobody likes being spoken to like they're clueless. Even if you are familiar with a topic, don't assume the other person is unfamiliar with it. Instead of launching into an explanation like you're the expert of the universe, check in first.

Example:
Respectful: "Are you familiar with how this works, or would you like me to explain?"

Condescending: "Oh, you probably don't know this, but let me tell you..."

Quick Fix:
Give people a chance to show what they know before offering advice.

3. Listen More Than You Talk
One of the fastest ways to sound condescending is to dominate the conversation. People feel respected when they feel heard.

Example:
Respectful: "That's interesting. What do you think about it?"
Condescending: "Well, the right way to look at this is..."
Nobody likes a conversation hijacker. Let people share their thoughts instead of waiting for your speech.

Quick Fix:
Listen to understand, not just to respond. Don't immediately jump in with corrections or your version of the story if someone shares something.

4. Be Careful with Compliments
Have you ever had someone "compliment" you in a way that felt more like an insult? That's called a backhanded compliment, and it's a classic way respect turns into condescension.

Example:
Respectful: "You did a great job on that project. I can tell you put a lot of effort into it."

Condescending: "Wow! I didn't expect you to do so well on that project. You surprised me!" See how the second one accidentally suggests that they weren't capable before?

Quick Fix:
When complimenting someone, focus on their effort, skills, or results, rather than your expectations.

5. Don't Over-Explain
There's a fine line between being helpful and treating someone like they're helpless. Over-explaining occurs when we assume someone won't understand something before they ask a question.

Example:
Respectful: "Let me know if you have any questions. I'm happy to help." Condescending: "Okay, first, you must open the app. Do you know how to do that? Next, you tap this button; it's the one that says 'Start.'" (Meanwhile, the other person is already three steps ahead of you.)

Quick Fix:
Check first! "Would you like me to walk you through it?" is always better than assuming they need a step-by-step manual.

6. Respect Different Opinions
One of the biggest mistakes people make is thinking their way is the only way and acting like they're handing out wisdom from the mountaintop.

Example:
Respectful: "I see it differently, but I get where you're coming from." Condescending: "Well, once you understand more about this, you'll see it my way." Nothing stops a conversation faster than acting like the other person needs more knowledge to come around to your side.

Quick Fix:
Respect that different people have different experiences and perspectives. You can share your view without making it sound like the only right one.

7. Be Aware of Your Body Language
Sometimes, it's not your words. It's your face. Eye rolls, raised eyebrows, smirks, slow nods, or even overly dramatic pauses can make a regular comment condescending.

Example:
Respectful: A usual nod and neutral expression while listening. Condescending: Smirking, raising an eyebrow, tilting your head like you're humouring them.

Quick Fix:
Keep your facial expressions relaxed and engaged, not amused or skeptical.

8. Know When to Keep Your Advice to Yourself
Not everyone is looking for a lesson. Sometimes, people share their thoughts without getting unsolicited advice.

Example:
Respectful: "That's interesting! I hadn't thought of it that way."
Condescending: "You know what you should do? You should try..."

Quick Fix:
Before giving advice, ask: "Would you like my thoughts on that?" If they say no, respect it.

Respect Comes from Authenticity

Authenticity is the key to being respectful without coming across as condescending. If your kindness is genuine, people will feel it. If your respect is genuine, it will be evident. Condescension sneaks in when we try too hard to sound intelligent, helpful, or superior. Remember, genuine respect is not just a social nicety; it's a powerful tool for building meaningful connections.

So, next time you're in a conversation, remember that respect isn't about showing how much you know; it's about showing how much you care.

Now, what do you think? Have you ever caught yourself slipping into a condescending tone without realizing it? Take a moment to reflect on your own experiences. Self-awareness and introspection can truly improve our communication skills.

TO DRESS TO EXPRESS SUCCESS

Donald: I'll take care of this part, okay Sweetheart?

Colleen: Of course, Baby.

Donald: Before we get into it, I want to take a quick moment to talk about something important, how you DON'T dress for a date. Unless you're trying to stay single. You ready? Alright, here it is: By a Woman Who's Seen Too Much and Said Too Little Until Now. Let's be honest. The clothes you wear on a date say something before you even open your mouth. Unfortunately, some men's outfits scream, "I had ten minutes and zero effort to spare." So, if you're out here wondering why your date ended early or why she "suddenly remembered" she had to walk her neighbour's dog, read on.

1. The Wrinkle Warrior
If your shirt looks like it was balled up at the bottom of the laundry basket and slept on by a cat, don't wear it.

Pro Tip: If you have to ask, "Is this too wrinkled?" it is. Iron it. Or better yet, learn how to iron. It's not black magic; it's adulting.

2. The Cologne Cloud
A light spritz is sexy. Bathing in it? Not so much. If your scent arrives five minutes before you do, we have a problem. You're on a date, not gassing out mosquitoes.

Pro Tip: One spritz, maybe two, on your skin, not your clothes. You're supposed to be irresistible, not flammable.

3. The Tightrope Walker

Pants so tight they threaten circulation? Jackets that won't button without prayer? That's not fashion; that's a cry for help.

Pro Tip: Tailor does not mean torture. Wear clothes that fit the man you are, not the teenager you were.

4. The Graphic Tee Gamble

Unless you're dating at an arcade, leave the "I flexed, and the sleeves fell off" T-shirt at home.

Pro tip: Go with a crisp button-down or a clean, well-fitted polo. Respect the moment. Show up like you want to be there.

5. Shoe Confusion

Crocs? Flip-flops? Scuffed-up sneakers from 2009? Just no.

Pro Tip: Invest in a solid pair of dress shoes or loafers. Your shoes speak before you make sure they're saying something worth hearing.

Now for a Quick Style Redemption List:

- A crisp button-down or clean polo shirt? Yes, sir.
- Well-fitted jeans or slacks that sit on your waist? Praise hands.
- Clean shoes? Automatic points.
- A blazer that doesn't cut off circulation? You're halfway to hero status.
- Groomed hair and beard, or clean-shaven, just pick a lane
- Subtle accessories: watch, belt, confidence
- The golden rule: Dress like you know she's worth the effort, and so are you.

Most importantly? Confidence. Not cockiness, not cologne overdose confidence, just "I know who I am, and I showed up for you" energy. Trust me, that never goes out of style.

Straight up:
What you wear on the outside reflects how much you care about what's happening on the inside. And if you can't dress like the date matters, don't be surprised when she decides you don't. Okay let's move on, I think you've gotten the gist of this little segment.

Grooming Habits That Elevate Your Presence
Let's be honest: First impressions matter. We like to think the world sees us for who we are on the inside, and sure, that's true eventually. But before we even open our mouths, our presence speaks for us. How we dress and groom is a silent introduction, a personal brand, and a message that says, "This is who I am." Now, don't get me wrong, this isn't about being flashy or following trends just for the sake of it.

Dressing to express success is about presenting yourself with intention. It's about refining your presence so that people feel your confidence before you say a word when you walk into a room. Success isn't just about what you do, but also about how you show up. The way you dress and groom yourself is a direct reflection of the standards you set for yourself. Let's discuss the simple yet powerful habits that can elevate your presence and ensure your style always speaks volumes.

1. Success Starts with Cleanliness - Nothing, and I mean nothing, elevates your presence faster than good hygiene. No one takes a business leader, entrepreneur, or professional seriously if they smell like yesterday's regrets. A fresh shower, clean nails, and well-kept hair are the foundation of a polished appearance. Smelling fresh and feeling clean isn't just about others; it's about you. When you take the time to care for yourself, you naturally carry yourself with more confidence. And trust me, people notice.

2. Grooming is a Daily Investment in Your Image - Some people think grooming is for special occasions such as weddings, interviews, or big meetings. Wrong. Grooming is a daily discipline; successful people know consistency is key. Every detail counts, whether maintaining your hair, keeping your beard sharp, or ensuring your skin is hydrated. A well-groomed individual gives the impression of discipline and self-respect. And let's be real: when you look put together, you feel put together, and that confidence translates into success.

3. The Power of a Perfect Fit - Success isn't about labels; it's about fit. You could buy the most expensive outfit in the store, but if it doesn't fit properly, it won't work. Tailoring is the secret weapon of stylish, successful individuals. Whether it's a power suit, a casual blazer, or a simple dress, how your clothes fit can make all the difference. Clothes that drape well and complement your shape show that you understand the art of presentation. Baggy, ill-fitting clothes? They whisper carelessly. But clothes that fit like they were made for you? They declare confidence, competence, and readiness, putting you in control of your professional image.

4. Shoes: The Foundation of a Strong Presence - You can tell a lot about a person by their shoes. Worn-out sneakers, scuffed dress shoes, or unpolished boots send the wrong message. The right shoes instantly elevate your look. Whether it's classic leather shoes, stylish boots, or sleek sneakers, keep them clean and in good condition. People look at your feet, so make sure they tell the right story. Remember, a polished look from head to toe is a signal of success, so be aware of your overall appearance.

5. Hair & Beard: Frame Your Face with Authority - Your hair is one of the first things people notice, whether long, short, curly, or straight. The secret? Keep it intentional. A great haircut tailored to your face shape and lifestyle makes all the difference. And for those with beards, grooming is a must. A sharp beard adds character, but an unkempt one? Well, let's say it doesn't scream "executive presence." Take the time to shape, trim, and care for it. A well-groomed face shows you take pride in your appearance, a trait of every successful person.

6. Your Signature Style: The Mark of Success - Dressing to express success is about creating a signature look that represents you. Maybe it's a love for bold accessories, a preference for classic neutrals, or a touch of vintage flair. Whatever it is, own it. Find colours that flatter you, silhouettes that make you feel unstoppable, and details that make your style yours. It's not about copying others but refining what makes you stand out. Your style should say, "I know who I am and where I'm going."

7. Presence: The Invisible Suit of Power - Ever notice how some people own a room? It's not just their clothes; it's their presence. Good posture, a firm handshake, and a confident walk elevate your look. You can wear the best outfit in the world, but if you slouch and shuffle, it loses its impact. Stand tall. Walk like you belong wherever you are. Your presence should be as sharp as your style.

8. Invest in Quality Over Quantity - A wardrobe packed with cheap, trendy clothes will never outshine a carefully curated collection of well-made essentials. Successful people invest in timeless pieces: a great jacket, a crisp white shirt, well-fitted jeans, and classic shoes. Fewer but better-quality items ensure you always look polished without trying too hard. Remember: quality speaks for itself.

9. Accessories: The Silent Power Move - Accessories are the secret ingredient to personal style. A sleek watch, a well-chosen pair of sunglasses, or a statement piece of jewelry can take your look from basic to refined. The key? Keep it tasteful. A little goes a long way. Overloading with accessories can look chaotic, but the right piece can make you unforgettable. The best accessories don't just add style; they add presence.

Essentials of a Gentleman's Wardrobe - Gentlemen, let's talk style. Not fashion; style. Fashion fades, trends come and go, but a gentleman's style? That's timeless. When you step out the door, your clothes aren't just fabric stitched together; they're a statement. It's about owning your look, choosing quality over quantity, and ensuring that when you step into a room, your style says, "I know who I am, and I know where I'm going." Now, before you roll your eyes and say, "I'm not into fashion," understand this: It's about expressing confidence, self-respect, and success before you even say a word.

Think about it: when you see a man dressed sharp, well-groomed, and carrying himself with presence, what do you assume? He's got his act together. He's confident. He's someone to pay attention to. That's the power of dressing to express success. It's not about clothes; it's about making a statement without having to speak. So, let's break down once again the essentials of a gentleman's wardrobe, the pieces that will ensure you're dressed to express success.

1. The Power Suit: Your Armour for Success - Every gentleman needs a perfectly tailored suit, no exceptions. A suit isn't just an outfit; it's a transformative tool. It says, "I take myself seriously, and so should you." Whether for a business meeting, a formal event, or a date where you want to impress, a well-fitted suit is your best friend, empowering you with confidence and a sense of readiness.

What to look for:
- Navy or Charcoal Gray – These colours work for almost any occasion.
- Tailored Fit – Baggy suits are a no-go. Get it fitted to your body.
- Classic Over Flashy – Avoid extreme patterns or loud colours if you want a timeless style.

And remember: a good tailor is your secret weapon. Off-the-rack can only take you so far; fit is everything.

2. Crisp White Dress Shirt: The Backbone of Your Wardrobe
A well-pressed, high-quality white dress shirt is the definition of effortless sophistication. Pair it with anything, such as a suit, chinos, or jeans, and instantly elevate your look.

Make sure it's:
- Slim or Regular Fit – No excess fabric hanging off the sides.
- High-Quality Cotton – Breathable and comfortable.
- Well-Ironed – Wrinkles are not your friend.

Pro tip: Always have at least three in your wardrobe: one for wearing, one in the wash, and one ready to go.

3. Dark Denim: Casual Yet Refined
A gentleman knows how to dress down without looking sloppy. Enter dark denim, the perfect balance between casual and put-together. Unlike light-wash jeans, which can look too relaxed, dark denim pairs well with blazers, sweaters, and even dress shoes.

Look for:
- Dark Indigo or Black – Timeless and versatile.
- Slim (Not Skinny) Fit – Too tight is a fashion statement. Too loose is lazy.
- Minimal Details – No crazy distressing, rips, or oversized logos.

Dark denim is perfect for dinner dates, casual Fridays, or weekend outings, wherever you want to look sharp without being overdressed.

4. The Classic Blazer: Instant Elegance

A blazer is the secret to looking effortlessly refined. Throw one over a T-shirt and jeans, and suddenly, you've gone from "just another guy" to "man of presence."

Essentials:
- Navy or Gray – Versatile and works with most outfits.
- Structured but Not Stiff – Find one that moves with you.
- Unbutton When You Sit – (Trust me, it looks better.)

Owning a great blazer means you're always one step away from looking sharp, no matter the occasion.

5. Leather Dress Shoes: The Mark of a Gentleman

You can tell everything about a man by his shoes. You could be wearing a $3,000 suit, but if your shoes are scuffed and worn out, that's all anyone will notice.

Must-haves:
- Oxford or Derby Shoes – Perfect for formal occasions.
- Brown Brogues or Loafers – Ideal for business casual or smart casual occasions.
- Polish Regularly – Keep them clean and in shape.

- Invest in quality leather shoes, and they'll last you for years. Plus, nothing beats the sound of a confident step in well-made shoes.

6. The Signature Watch: A Gentleman's Timepiece
A man's watch is more than just a timepiece; it reflects his personality. It's a subtle yet powerful accessory that ties his whole look together.

What to consider:
- Classic and Minimalist – A simple, clean face always looks sophisticated.
- Leather or Metal Band – Select the one that best matches your style.
- Too Flashy – Keep the diamonds to a minimum unless you're a rapper.
- A good watch says, "I value time: myself and you."

7. A Versatile Overcoat: The Final Layer of Success
Cold weather is no excuse to let your style slip. A well-fitted overcoat ensures you look sharp while staying warm.

Best choices:
- Wool or Cashmere Blend – Classic and durable.
- Camel, Navy, or Charcoal – Timeless colours.
- Fits Over Your Suit – Make enough room for layering.
- An overcoat isn't just a necessity; it's a power move.

8. The Leather Belt: The Small Detail That Ties It All
A belt isn't just there to hold up your pants; it completes your look.

Golden rule: Your belt should always match your shoes.
- Black belt for black shoes.

- Brown belt for brown shoes.

A gentleman's essential finishing touch is a quality leather belt with a simple, elegant buckle.

9. The Pocket Square: Small Yet Powerful
A pocket square is one of those details that separates the stylish from the ordinary. It's a small piece of fabric, but it adds a great deal of personality to a suit or blazer.

- Crisp White for Classic Elegance
- Patterned for a Bit of Flair
- Fold It Neatly (No Stuffing It In)

It's a tiny touch, but trust me, it gets noticed.

Just one more thing: The Right Fragrance: Your Signature
Dressing for success isn't just about what people see; it's also about what they sense. A pleasing fragrance leaves a lasting impression. Choose a subtle, masculine cologne that enhances your presence without overpowering the room. The goal is to intrigue, not to announce yourself from across the street.

Confidence: The True Secret to Dressing for Success
Grooming and style truly elevate your presence. You can wear the sharpest suit, the finest shoes, and the best cologne, but it doesn't matter if you don't own your look. For instance, a well-groomed beard, a neatly tied tie, and a polished pair of shoes can make a significant difference. A gentleman's wardrobe is a tool, not a crutch.

If you want success, start by looking the part. But remember, it's not just about how others see you; it's about how you see yourself. Walk into every room like you belong there. Show up for yourself first, and success will follow. Walk tall. Speak with purpose. Shake hands firmly. Smile. Because at the end of the day, success isn't just about how you dress; it's about how you carry yourself in everything you do.

Dressing to express success isn't about vanity; it's about vision. It's about presenting yourself as the man you know you are and the man you aspire to be. When you dress with intention, you're not just putting on clothes but stepping into a new version of yourself. People take you seriously, opportunities open up, and your presence commands respect. So, gentlemen, dress not just for the moment but for the success you're stepping into. And when you dress to express success, you're already halfway there.

So, ask yourself: Are you dressing for where you are or for where you want to be? The world is watching; what will your wardrobe say about you? A gentleman's wardrobe is more than just fabric and fashion; it's a mirror that reflects your ambition, respect, and the success you strive for.

The Art of Dressing: Mastering the Power of Presentation
To finish up on dressing to express success, let's talk about how we live in a world where first impressions matter. Whether we like it or not, people judge us within seconds of meeting us. Our appearance speaks before we do, setting the tone for how we are perceived, respected, and treated. Dressing appropriately for different occasions is not about self-importance but strategy. It's about understanding that presentation is a powerful tool influencing opportunities, relationships, and even our self-confidence.

Clothing as a Language
Think of fashion as a silent conversation. Once again, how we dress tells a story about who we are, what we value, and how seriously we take the situation. If you step into a business meeting in ripped jeans and sneakers, you send a message of

casual indifference. If you arrive at a wedding in an elegant ensemble, you communicate respect for the couple's special day. Every setting has its unspoken dress code; mastering it gives you an undeniable advantage.

Dressing appropriately is not about conforming to rigid rules or sacrificing individuality; it's about aligning your external presence with the energy and expectations of the environment. A polished look doesn't just make you look good; it empowers you, giving you a sense of control over your perception.

The Power of Presentation in Professional Settings
Your wardrobe choices can open or close doors in your career. Studies show that people who dress well in the workplace are more likely to be perceived as competent, trustworthy, and capable. This does not mean you need to wear expensive designer clothing, but you should dress in a way that reflects professionalism, confidence, and ambition.

Consider two candidates applying for the same job. One arrives in a well-tailored suit, hair neatly groomed, and shoes polished. The other shows up in a wrinkled shirt and ill-fitting pants. Who leaves a stronger impression? The answer is obvious. Dressing well demonstrates that you respect yourself and the opportunity in front of you. It signals to employers, clients, and colleagues that you are serious about your ambitions.

Even in creative industries, where dress codes are more relaxed, there is a delicate balance between expressing personality and maintaining professionalism. A designer wearing bold prints and trendy accessories still conveys a curated, intentional look. It is never just about the clothes; it's about the thoughts behind them. Your style can be a powerful tool in these settings, allowing you to stand out while still fitting in.

Social Occasions: Dressing with Respect and Confidence
Beyond the workplace, dressing appropriately plays a vital role in our social lives. Imagine casually attending a black-tie event or wearing beachwear to a fancy dinner. These missteps are not just fashion faux pas; they can make you feel out of place and uncomfortable. A formal evening gown or a tuxedo would be more appropriate for a black-tie event. When we dress harmoniously with the occasion, we step into the moment confidently and efficiently.

Dressing well in social settings is a way of showing respect for others. When you take the time to present yourself well, it communicates, 'I value being here. I appreciate this event, and I respect those around me.' This applies to everything from weddings and celebrations to casual gatherings with friends. Dressing with intention not only enhances your presence but also your social confidence.

I'll never forget this one business event my boyfriend and I attended. We both love dressing to express success; that night was no exception. The moment we walked in, heads turned. People assumed we were the owners or major investors behind the event! But it wasn't just about the clothes; we carry ourselves confidently, and that energy is magnetic. People are naturally curious; no matter where we go, we want to know who we are and what we do. That's the power of presentation; it speaks before you even say a word.

The Psychological Impact of Dressing Well
The most potent effect of presentation is its influence on our mindset. What we wear affects how we carry ourselves, how we interact with others, and even how we perform tasks. Psychologists call this 'enclothed cognition,' the idea that what we wear influences our behaviour, attitudes, and confidence

levels. Dressing well can make you feel more confident and capable, ready to take on any challenge.

Have you ever noticed how wearing a well-fitted outfit instantly boosts your confidence? How does a power suit make you taller, or how does a beautiful dress make you feel radiant? That is the magic of presentation. Dressing well is not about impressing others; it is about aligning with the best version of yourself.

Striking the Right Balance: Personal Style Meets Occasion
While it is essential to dress appropriately for each setting, personal style should never be sacrificed. The goal is not to conform mindlessly but to blend authenticity with awareness. A person who loves bold colours and statement jewelry can still exude professionalism by incorporating those elements into a well-structured outfit. A minimalist dresser can still shine at a gala by choosing sleek, elegant pieces. The key is to respect the setting while staying true to yourself.

Own Your Presentation, Own Your Power
In conclusion, dressing appropriately for different occasions concerns fashion, presence, preparation, and personal power. It's about showing up as your best self, ready to welcome the opportunities that come your way. Remember, how you present yourself reflects your self-respect, confidence, and understanding of the world around you. And when you dress with intention, you not only impress others, but you also inspire yourself. So, own your presentation, own your power.

Your wardrobe is your armour, your introduction, and your silent ambassador. Make it count. Whether stepping into a boardroom, attending a wedding, or simply heading out for a casual brunch, remember this: how you present yourself reflects your self-respect, confidence, and understanding of the world around you. And when you dress with intention, you do not just impress others; you inspire yourself.

THE ART OF DINING

Colleen: Hey, Babe, my turn.

Donald: Definitely yours.

Why Table Manners Matter

Colleen: Welcome to a lesson in refinement, confidence, and the art of dining. Dining is not just about eating; it is a graceful performance, a statement of elegance, and an opportunity to present yourself as a person of grace, sophistication, and respect. Whether you're sharing a meal with business associates, a date, or attending a formal event, your table manners speak volumes about your character and leave a lasting impression.

Picture this: She walks into a fine-dining restaurant, the candlelit ambiance setting the mood for an elegant evening. A well-dressed gentleman stands as she approaches. He pulls out a chair for her and waits until she is seated before taking his place. He folds his napkin with ease, engages in effortless conversation, and navigates the table setting with quiet confidence that speaks volumes.

As you know, I teach men how to personify the essence of a gentleman through *The "MR" Factor*: Mastery and Refinement. Mastery refers to the skill and knowledge you possess, while refinement is about the elegance and sophistication you display.

These two key elements extend beyond how you speak, dress, or carry yourself. They shine through even how you handle a fork, sip your drink, or converse while dining. A gentleman doesn't just eat; he dines with purpose, elegance, and an understanding that his presence at the table is as much a reflection of his character as his words and actions.

In today's fast-paced world, many have dismissed etiquette as old-fashioned, an unnecessary set of rules reserved for the elite. But let me tell you, mastering dining etiquette is not about snobbery; it is about self-respect, confidence, and the ability to leave a lasting impression. Whether at a corporate dinner, a first date, or an elegant gala, how you conduct yourself at the table speaks volumes about your character.

If you're a man striving to personify *The "MR" Factor,* Mastery, and Refinement, understanding the nuances of proper dining is non-negotiable. A man who master's the art of dining commands respect. When you command respect, you create opportunities, build meaningful relationships, and exude a presence that leaves a lasting impression.

The fork, the knife, and the napkin are just tools; the authentic elegance comes from the man using them. So, sit up straight, unfold your napkin, and let me guide you through the art of table manners with the elegance and ease of a true gentleman.

The Essentials of Table Manners

1. The Art of Sitting and Presence at the Table
Before we even touch the cutlery, let's talk about presence. A gentleman doesn't slump into his chair or sprawl across the table as if claiming territory. Instead, he sits upright yet relaxed, exuding confidence without arrogance.

- When taking your seat, enter from the right and sit down gracefully, not flopping or dragging the chair noisily.
- Keep both feet on the floor and avoid leaning on the table like a crutch.
- Napkin placement: When seated, unfold your napkin and place it on your lap. It stays there throughout the meal, unless you need to excuse yourself, so you put it neatly on your chair.
- This level of awareness might seem small, but trust me, it leaves a lasting impression.

2. Handling Your Utensils Like a Gentleman
The way you handle your cutlery speaks volumes. There is an art to using a knife and fork that goes beyond simply shoveling food into your mouth.

- Continental vs. American Style: In European dining etiquette, the fork stays in the left hand, and the knife remains in the right throughout the meal. In American etiquette, you cut your food and then switch your fork to your right hand to eat. Either style is acceptable, but stabbing your food like a caveman is unacceptable.
- Proper cutting technique: Cut one bite at a time, not your entire steak, as if preparing it for a toddler. A gentleman savours his meal; he doesn't pre-chop it like an assembly line worker.
- Holding utensils with finesse: Avoid gripping your knife like a dagger. Hold it relaxed, with your index finger gently guiding the blade. Your fork should not resemble a pitchfork; use only the necessary amount of pressure to pick up food gracefully.
- Refinement is in the details, gentlemen.

3. Eating with Elegance
Now, let's talk about the actual act of eating.

- Chew with your mouth closed. This should be common sense, but it bears repeating, nonetheless.
- Take small bites. No one needs to witness you stuffing an entire bread roll into your mouth in one go.
- Do not talk with food in your mouth. A conversation can wait a few seconds while you finish chewing.
- Sip, don't slurp. No one wants to hear the sound of suction in soup, coffee, or wine.
- Dining etiquette is not just about the individual; it's about being considerate of those around you and making the dining experience enjoyable for everyone. It's about respecting the food, the setting, and the people you're dining with. It's about being mindful of your actions and their impact on yourself and the entire dining experience.

4. Mastering Conversation at the Table
The "MR" Factor isn't just about how you eat; it's also about how you engage with those around you. A true gentleman understands that dining is a social affair.

- Engage in balanced conversation. A true gentleman does not dominate the discussion or fade into the background. Show interest in others, ask thoughtful questions, and be genuinely present.
- Remember, dining is a social affair, and your engagement can enhance the experience for everyone at the table. Topics to avoid: Religion, politics, and controversial issues are best left for another setting. Keep the conversation light, engaging, and pleasant.
- Listen attentively. Do not interrupt others mid-sentence; for heaven's sake, do not check your phone

at the table. The person in front of you deserves your full attention.
- Being a gentleman means being both an excellent speaker and a respectful listener.

5. Navigating Formal Dining with Ease
Seeing multiple forks, knives, and glasses might be intimidating if you ever find yourself at a formal dinner. But fear not; there's a simple rule to follow work from the outside.

- The utensils farthest from your plate are for the earlier courses.
- Bread plates are to your left, and drink glasses to your right.
- Never reach across the table; ask politely for items to be passed.
- And remember, a gentleman never rushes through a meal. He dines with patience, appreciating the flavours and the company.

6. The Drinking Code: Stemware and Confidence
Wine glasses have stems for a reason; hold them by the stem to avoid warming the drink. Water? Continuously sip before wine. And gentlemen, never guzzle. Take measured, intentional sips.

7. Common Table Faux Pas (And How to Avoid Them)
Another reminder of the mistakes that separate a polished man from a careless one:

- Reaching across the table – Politely ask someone to pass on what you need.
- Slouching or placing elbows on the table – Sit straight; posture speaks volumes.
- Talking with a full mouth – It's essential but often ignored.

- Checking your phone – Keep it away unless it's an emergency. Giving your full attention is a sign of respect.
- Seasoning before tasting – It's an insult to the chef; try the dish as it was prepared first.

The Final Touch: Exiting with Grace
Once the meal ends, resist the urge to push your plate away or stack dishes; that's the server's job, not yours. Instead:
- Place your knife and fork together on the plate at the 4 o'clock, signaling you are finished.
- Dab your mouth with your napkin (don't wipe aggressively), then place it beside your plate.
- Thank your host or server with genuine appreciation.
- A gentleman leaves the table as he arrives gracefully and with presence.

Bringing It All Together
The *"MR" Factor* is about more than just good manners; it's about Mastery and Refinement in every aspect of your presence, including how you conduct yourself at the table. When you demonstrate exceptional dining etiquette, you set yourself apart as a man of sophistication, respect, and confidence.

So, the next time you sit down for a meal, remember that dining is an experience, not just a function. Your table manners are your silent introduction. Let them speak well of you.

Now, gentlemen, go forth and dine with distinction.

MASTERING THE ART OF INTRODUCTION

Let me ask you a question: When you introduce yourself, do you leave a lasting impression or become another forgettable face in the crowd? A gentleman understands that introductions are not just a formality but an opportunity. How you introduce yourself and others determines the tone of the conversation, the level of respect you command, and the impression you leave behind.

I will teach you how to introduce yourself and others by implementing *The "MR" Factor*, a powerful approach that ensures you exude confidence, gain respect, and make meaningful connections. This isn't about just stating your name and shaking hands; it's about mastering a skill that will elevate your social presence, whether in business, social gatherings, or everyday interactions. So, gentlemen, let's get to work.

The Power of First Impressions
Before we deal with technique, let's get one thing straight: People decide who you are within seconds of meeting you. Before you even say a complete sentence, they have already formed an opinion about you based on your posture, demeanour, and confidence in your voice.

If you introduce yourself with uncertainty, hesitation, or a weak handshake, you've already lost ground. But if you walk in with the presence of a man who belongs, speaks with purpose, and carries himself with confidence, you set the tone for how others will perceive you. And this, gentlemen, is where *The "MR" Factor* comes into play.

Understanding *The "MR" Factor* in Introductions is your key to making strong, memorable introductions. It stands for:

- Mannerisms – The way you present yourself before and during introductions.
- Respect – The way you introduce others and acknowledge their presence.

When you master these two elements, introductions become seamless, powerful, and effective. Let's break it down step by step.

Step One: Introducing Yourself with Confidence
When you introduce yourself, your goal is to make a strong first impression. Here's how:

1. Master Your Body Language
- Stand tall. Posture matters. Keep your shoulders back, chest open, and feet firmly planted.
- Make eye contact. Looking someone directly in the eyes while introducing yourself conveys confidence and sincerity.
- Offer a firm handshake. A weak or limp handshake suggests insecurity, while an overly aggressive one can seem domineering. The perfect handshake is firm, not forceful.

2. Perfect Your Verbal Introduction
What you say matters just as much as how you say it. Here's the formula for introducing yourself properly:
- Say your full name clearly and confidently. Avoid mumbling or rushing through your name.
- State your purpose or role if appropriate. If you're in a professional setting, follow up with a brief statement about your role and responsibilities.
- Engage with a follow-up question. Confidence is about control. Instead of saying, "I'm John Smith," follow it with a relevant comment or question.

For example:
Weak Introduction: "Uh, hi. I'm John." (Forgettable and uncertain.)

Strong Introduction: "Good evening, I'm John Smith. I've heard great things about this event. How do you know the host?" (Confident and engaging.)

A confident introduction is clear, intentional, and engaging.

Step Two: Introducing Others the Right Way
As a gentleman, you often find yourself in situations where you must introduce two people. This is where social intelligence and *The "MR" Factor* set you apart.

A proper introduction isn't just about saying names; it's about making both parties feel valued and connected.

1. Prioritize the Most Distinguished Person
When introducing two people, always say the higher-ranking person's name first.

For example:
If introducing a friend to your boss, say:
"Mr. Thompson, I'd like to introduce my colleague, David. David, this is Mr. Thompson, the head of our department."

This demonstrates respect while ensuring that both parties feel acknowledged.

2. Provide Context to Build Connection
Simply stating names is not enough; give people something to connect over.

For Example:
Basic Introduction: "Mark, this is Sarah. Sarah, this is Mark."

Confident Introduction: "Mark, I'd love for you to meet Sarah, she's an expert in marketing and has done incredible work in digital branding. Sarah, Mark is one of the sharpest business strategists I know."

See the difference? Instead of just exchanging names, you've created a genuine and engaging connection.

3. Use Titles and Proper Forms of Address
Until given permission, always use formal titles when introducing someone of higher status, age, or rank.

For example:
"Dr. Lewis, may I introduce my friend Michael?"
"Senator Roberts, this is David, a colleague of mine in the finance industry."

This level of respect leaves a lasting impression.

Step Three: Exiting an Introduction Gracefully

Knowing how to exit an introduction is just as important as knowing how to start one. If the conversation naturally progresses, great. But if you need to move on, do so smoothly and with class.

Here's how to exit without awkwardness:

Acknowledge both parties with gratitude.
"It was a pleasure meeting you both. I hope you have a fantastic evening."

Give a reason if necessary.
"I'd love to continue this conversation, but I need to catch up with a colleague before the event ends. Let's connect later."

Leave with confidence. There was no hesitation, no fumbling, just a smooth exit.

Why This Matters
A gentleman doesn't just blend into a crowd; he stands out because he can effortlessly engage with others. Proper introductions are not just about etiquette; they are about building relationships, earning respect, and positioning yourself as a leader. By implementing *The "MR" Factor*, you will:

- Make lasting first impressions.
- Show respect in every interaction.
- Build stronger, more meaningful connections.

Confidence is built in the details, gentlemen. And the particulars begin with how you introduce yourself and others. So, how will you introduce yourself today?

SOCIAL SETTINGS WITH CONFIDENCE

Please pull up a chair, pour yourself a glass of sophistication, and let's talk about something that will set you apart from the crowd: the art of navigating social settings with confidence. If you've ever walked into a room and felt unsure of how to present yourself, command respect without demanding it, or leave an impression long after you've exited, you're exactly where you need to be.

Today, I'm here to guide you on a transformative journey, teaching you how to implement *The "MR" Factor*, a powerful framework designed to help you master presence, polish, and poise. This isn't just about looking the part; it's about being the part. It's about developing a distinguished presence that people naturally gravitate toward you. Confidence is not arrogance; it's assurance. It's a silent strength; a knowingness you belong wherever you set foot. And gentlemen, that is precisely what we're here to cultivate.

Understanding The "MR" Factor
Before we discuss the strategies, let's clarify one thing: confidence is not something you "have" or "don't have." It's built, shaped, and refined. With *The "MR" Factor*, it becomes second nature.

Step One: The Power of Mannerisms
Confidence begins before you even say a word. Think of historical figures like Winston Churchill, Martin Luther King Jr., or Terry Fox, who could command a room simply by stepping into it. What do they all have in common? Presence. And presence begins with mannerisms.

Mastering Posture & Movement
A man who slouches, fidgets, or shifts uncomfortably in social settings unknowingly broadcasts uncertainty. To be perceived as confident, you must first feel convinced, starting with how you stand, sit, and move.

- Stand tall, shoulders back, chest open. This isn't about puffing up like a rooster but creating a posture that signals self-assurance.
- Walk with purpose. Your steps should be deliberate, whether entering a restaurant, a business meeting, or a social gathering. No hesitation, no aimless wandering; move as if you belong.
- Make eye contact, not aggressively, but in a way that communicates presence and engagement. A man

holding eye contact without looking away too quickly commands attention.

The Art of Gestures
Your hands tell a story before your mouth ever does. A confident man is measured in his gestures, controlled, intentional, and never excessive.

- Use your hands to emphasize points, not to fidget.
- Avoid crossing your arms; this creates a barrier between you and the people you engage with.
- Practice stillness. A man who is comfortable in silence, without unnecessary movements, radiates quiet strength.

Step Two: The Currency of Respect
Confidence means nothing if it isn't backed by respect. A true gentleman understands that respect is both earned and given. Respect in Conversation A confident man doesn't dominate a conversation; he guides, engages, and enhances it. Here's how:

- Listen more than you speak. Nothing exudes confidence like the ability to listen attentively. When someone is talking, be present. Absorb their words before responding.
- Avoid interrupting. Confidence is knowing your turn will come without forcing it.
- Speak with intention. Choose your words wisely. Please don't rush to fill the silence; let it work in your favour.
- A man who listens well, speaks purposefully and engages authentically commands attention effortlessly.

Respecting Social Hierarchies & Environments
Every social setting has its own unspoken rules and hierarchies. A confident man understands how to read and navigate a room, respecting the established social order and showing deference where appropriate.

- If you're in a formal setting, err on polished elegance; be courteous, measured, and deliberate in your interactions.
- In casual settings, confidence comes from ease, not exaggeration. Don't try too hard. Be relaxed but maintain self-awareness.
- Always introduce yourself with strength and clarity. A firm handshake, direct eye contact, and a self-assured tone go a long way.

Step Three: The Execution of Confidence
Confidence becomes second nature once you've mastered your mannerisms and established a sense of respect. Here's how to ensure your presence remains impactful:

Projecting Your Voice with Authority
Your voice is a tool, one that should convey calm control.

- Speak clearly and deliberately. Rushed speech suggests nervousness; controlled speech suggests confidence.
- Adjust your tone based on the setting. A lower, steady tone commands attention, while a varied, expressive tone keeps conversations engaging.
- Avoid filler words like 'um', 'uh', 'you know', or 'like'. Silence is more potent than these unnecessary words; eliminating them from your speech will make your communication more confident and impactful.

Mastering the Exit

A confident man knows how to leave an impression that lingers. Whether you're excited about a conversation or an entire event, do so with the same grace and strength you entered with. It's not about being the last to leave but about leaving a lasting impression.

- End conversations with a firm handshake and a memorable remark. ("It was a pleasure speaking with you. I look forward to our next conversation.")
- Depart without hesitation: no lingering, no awkward goodbyes, just a smooth, self-assured exit.
-

The "MR" Factor in Action

Imagine this: You step into a room. Your posture is strong, and your movements are intentional. You engage in conversation, listening more than you speak and responding with depth and insight. Your gestures are measured, and your words are deliberate. People remember you when you leave, not because you demanded attention but because your presence naturally commanded it. That, gentlemen, is *The "MR" Factor* in action.

Confidence Is a Choice

The key takeaway? Confidence isn't about being the loudest person in the room. It's about being the most composed, self-assured, and present. It's about navigating social settings with a gentleman's grace and a leader's quiet strength.

Confidence is a muscle; train it daily. Implement The MR Factor consistently, and soon, you will not only be navigating social settings but mastering them. So, tell me, gentlemen, how will you implement *The "MR" Factor* today?

THE "MR" FACTOR TRAVEL ETIQUETTE

In today's globalized world, travel has become more than just a means of transportation; it's an experience that speaks volumes about who we are as individuals. Whether traveling for business or leisure, how you conduct yourself while on the move reveals a great deal about your character.

As a man of distinction, embracing world-class travel etiquette is not just about following rules but mastering the art of leaving a lasting, positive impression everywhere. This is the essence of *The "MR" Factor* and is the key to behaving like a true world-class man.

1. Be Punctual, Always - Time is one of the most valuable commodities we all possess. A world-class man understands and always respects this principle, especially while traveling. Whether catching a flight, attending a meeting, or simply arriving at a social event, punctuality respects others' time. Being late can be considered inconsiderate, even if the delay is unavoidable. A world-class man plans ahead, ensures all logistics are in order, and arrives with time to spare. This behaviour signals to others that you value their presence and, most importantly, respect yourself. Your punctuality is not just a personal trait, but a sign of your responsibility and consideration for others.

2. Maintain Your Composure in Crowded Spaces - Airports, train stations, and other travel hubs can often feel like chaotic arenas of humanity. As a man who embodies *The "MR" Factor*, it's crucial to maintain your calm in such environments. Whether standing in line or navigating through a crowded space, it's essential to remain patient, respectful, and composed. Rushing, pushing, or showing frustration only adds to the tension around you. A world-class man can remain poised under pressure, demonstrating self-control and grace.

3. Mind Your Space and Belongings - When traveling, it's easy to get distracted by the hustle and bustle of getting to your next destination. However, a world-class man is always mindful of his personal space and the space of others. For instance, do not compromise others' comfort when seated on a plane, train, or bus. Keep your belongings neatly organized and avoid spreading out unnecessarily. Be mindful of others around you in confined spaces, such as hotel lobbies or waiting areas. Your actions reflect who you are, and a world-class man always strives to maintain a considerate and respectful presence.

4. Be Polite to Everyone, No Matter the Role - It's easy to be polite to those in positions of power or influence. However, a world-class man understands that true character is revealed in how he treats those who may not seem able to offer anything in return. Whether you're interacting with a flight attendant, hotel staff, or taxi driver, your level of respect should be the same. A simple "thank you" or "please" goes a long way in fostering goodwill. The way you treat others speaks volumes about your integrity and kindness. A world-class man is gracious, no matter the position or status of the person he's interacting with.

5. Dress the Part - A world-class man knows that appearance matters, especially when traveling. It's not about wearing a designer suit on every occasion; it's about selecting clothes that are suitable for the setting and reflect your personal style. A well-dressed man carries himself with confidence and class. Whether stepping off a plane, attending a business meeting, or simply walking into a café, your attire should be neat, well-fitted, and thoughtful. The proper attire doesn't just elevate your appearance; it also communicates to others that you care about the experience and understand the power of presentation. Your attire reflects your style and is a tool for effective communication and self-awareness.

6. Be Culturally Aware and Respectful - One of the most remarkable traits of a world-class man is his ability to adapt to various cultural norms and practices while traveling. Regardless of your location, take the time to understand the local customs, traditions, and etiquette. Whether it's a simple greeting or dining etiquette, demonstrating respect for the culture you're in shows sophistication and intelligence. A world-class man never imposes his cultural expectations on others. Instead, he embraces the world's diversity, learning from each new place he visits.

7. Stay Calm in the Face of Travel Mishaps - Let's face it: Travel is unpredictable. Flights get delayed, luggage gets lost, and plans don't always go smoothly. However, a world-class man handles such situations with composure and resilience. He stays calm and finds a solution rather than getting upset or venting his frustrations on others. His ability to remain calm under challenging situations sets him apart as a leader. Whether finding a new flight, politely asking for assistance, or simply taking a moment to reset, a world-class man turns travel mishaps into opportunities for grace and learning. Your ability to stay calm during travel mishaps shows your flexibility and adaptability.

The World-Class Man on the Move - *The "MR" Factor* isn't just about traveling in style; it's about embodying a standard of excellence and courtesy that leaves a lasting impact. From being punctual and respectful to dressing appropriately and handling mishaps gracefully, every action you take as a traveler reflects your character. As a man of distinction, you can turn every travel experience into a display of your world-class persona. Remember: it's not just where you go but how you go that defines you. So, the next time you step onto a plane, enter a new city, or navigate an unfamiliar culture, let your actions speak louder than words. Be the man who embodies *The "MR" Factor* wherever you go.

EMOTIONAL INTELLIGENCE & SELF-MASTERY

Mastering Emotions Like a True Gentleman
Let's talk about something: most men weren't given a manual for emotions. Before you roll your eyes and click away, hear me out. That's right, those pesky, powerful, sometimes unpredictable feelings that can either make or break you. You've mastered your career, hobbies, and even your sense of style. But have you mastered yourself?

The "MR" Factor isn't just about looking at the part of a gentleman; it's about being one inside and out. And that means understanding and managing emotions like the gentleman you were born to be.

Why Should You Care?
Let's be real: most men weren't taught how to process emotions properly. Society says, "Be strong, suck it up, keep moving, or real men don't cry." Because emotions are a sign of weakness, but here's the truth: real men do feel. And the strongest, most respected men know how to handle those emotions rather than letting them handle them.

Emotional intelligence separates the boys from the gentlemen, whether in your relationships, career, or personal growth. And sure, resilience is excellent, but suppressing emotions? That's a ticking time bomb. Unchecked anger turns into outbursts. Bottled-up sadness morphs into burnout. Ignored stress manifests in your health. And the worst part? It impacts your relationships, career, and overall well-being.

So, what if I told you that mastering your emotions is not just about feeling better; it's about winning in every aspect of your life? Because when you know how to manage your feelings, you command respect, gain confidence, and make decisions with clarity.

The Power of Emotional Intelligence (EQ)
Men are often taught to value IQ, brains, logic, and quick thinking. But EQ, or emotional intelligence, is just as important. It's about recognizing, understanding, and managing your emotions and those of others. The best leaders, partners, and professionals don't just know what to say; they know how to convey it effectively. They read the room. They adjust. They respond instead of reacting. That's what makes them magnetic, influential, and damn near unstoppable.

Understanding Your Emotional Compass
Before you can master emotions, you have to recognize them. Simple, right? Not always. Many men go through life suppressing or ignoring their feelings until they bubble over into anger or frustration. However, here's the thing: anger is often just a cover-up for deeper emotions, such as fear, hurt, or insecurity.

The key is learning to identify what's going on inside. Understanding your emotional compass: Every man has an emotional compass. It's just that some haven't learned how to read it yet. Here's the secret: Emotions aren't the enemy. They're signals.

- **Anger?** It's telling you something that feels unfair or out of control.
- **Fear?** It highlights uncertainty, risk, or the need for courage.

- **Sadness?** It reminds you of something valuable that's been lost.
- **Happiness?** It's a sign you're aligned with what matters.

Understanding these signals is the first step. Ignoring them is like driving without a GPS: You might still get somewhere, but you'll waste a lot of time taking the wrong turns. Try this: The next time you feel irritated or upset, pause for a moment. Ask yourself: What's bothering me? Is it stress? Is it disappointment? Is it fear of failure? Getting to the root of your emotions helps you deal with them before they become a problem.

Managing Emotions Like a Gentleman

Okay, so now you understand your emotions; great. But how do you control them? Here's the secret: It's not about suppressing them but channeling them correctly. Here's where The "MR" Factor comes in. Consider these six techniques:

1. **Breathe First:** React Later. Have you ever sent a text in the heat of the moment and regretted it later? That's your emotions hijacking your logic. When you feel overwhelmed, take a deep breath (or five). Give yourself space before you respond. A gentleman always thinks before he speaks.

2. **Master the Art of Composure:** Being emotionally intelligent doesn't mean venting like a soap opera character. The loudest guy in the room isn't the strongest. It's the one who can keep his cool. Whether it's a heated argument, a business negotiation, or a personal setback, composure is a powerful asset. Practice pausing before reacting. Confidence comes from control.

3. **Know When to Walk Away:** Not every battle is worth fighting. If a situation escalates beyond reason, disengaging is the most brilliant move. Walking away doesn't mean you're weak; it means you value your peace over unnecessary conflict.

4. **Own Your Feelings:** Blaming others for how you feel? That's a rookie move. "She made me mad" or "That guy ruined my day" takes the power out of your hands. Instead, say, "I felt frustrated when that happened." Ownership gives you control.

5. **Upgrade Your Emotional Vocabulary:** You're not just "mad" or "fine." There's a spectrum of emotions in between. The more you can name your feelings, the better you can deal with them. Are you frustrated, disappointed, or annoyed? Pinpoint it, and you'll handle it better.

6. **Master the Art of Emotional Reset:** Every man needs a mental reset button. Whether working out, playing an instrument, hitting the sauna, or taking a long drive, find what clears your mind. Emotionally intelligent men don't dwell; they reset and refocus. The more adaptable you are, the stronger you become.

Understanding Others' Emotions

Being emotionally intelligent isn't just about you; it's about how you connect with others. Want to be a man that people respect, trust, and admire? Learn to read emotions like a seasoned pro.

- **Listen More, talk less:** People don't just want to be heard; they want to be understood. Practice active listening, nodding, paraphrasing, and showing genuine interest in what someone is saying.

- **Empathy is a Strength, Not a Weakness:** Seeing things from another person's perspective makes you a better leader, friend, and partner. It shows maturity and depth.

- **Nonverbal Cues Matter:** People communicate more through body language and tone than words. Pay attention to crossed arms, averted eyes, or nervous gestures. They tell you more than you think.

The Gentleman's Edge

The "MR" Factor isn't about perfection; it's about awareness. A true gentleman knows that mastering emotions isn't a one-time thing; it's a lifelong practice.

That's the Master's Pillar: owning your growth and stepping up consistently.

Still not convinced? Here's the deal: A man who understands and manages his emotions stands out. He's respected in the boardroom. He's admired in his personal life. Women trust him. Other men seek his advice. Why? Emotional strength is a hallmark of authentic leadership. It's the difference between reacting like a boy and responding like a man.

And that emotional strength? That's Aure Chi in action, the heart-driven awareness that separates you from the average guy. So, ask yourself: Are you just existing or evolving? *The "MR" Factor* isn't about becoming someone else but being your best version. And that's a man worth being.

Becoming your best self means leveling up with Nobler standards, bringing dignity, class, and calm confidence into every room you enter. Here's the challenge: Start today. Pay attention to what you feel, how you react, and how you handle situations. The more you practice, the stronger and more composed you'll become. And that, my friend, is what makes a man truly extraordinary.

It's not about being perfect. It's about being present (Masters), emotionally tuned in (Aure Chi), and refined (Nobler) all at once. Ready to level up? The world needs more gentlemen who master their emotions. Are you in?

Colleen: I've always known I bring a steady kind of energy to the table, especially in a world that seems to shift under our feet daily. But let me tell you, having someone beside me like Don, who matches that energy with a quiet kind of strength? Game changer.

Donald: She says I've got that steady thing going, and I guess I do. But it's not some magic trick; I try to show up with honesty. No games, no guessing, just real talk. That's what keeps things solid.

Colleen: Communication is everything in a relationship: parent and child, best friends, siblings, lovers, you name it. And yeah, we have our moments. We're not perfect (who is?), but when we hit a rough patch, he doesn't shut down or sugarcoat. He speaks up. He speaks his truth.

Donald: I don't see the point in holding things in. If something's bothering me, I'd rather get it out there than let it fester. Yeah, it can be uncomfortable sometimes, but silence builds walls, and I'm not about that life.

Colleen: That kind of honesty? It can sting a little, I won't lie. But it also feels like a compass when the emotional fog rolls in. I'd rather deal with the sting of truth than wander in the dark wondering what's going on. With Don, I always know where we stand. That's a rare gift.

Donald: Look, emotions aren't just for poetry and drama. They're information. If you can't get a handle on your own feelings, how can you expect to connect with someone else? Real love needs real talk.

Colleen: Exactly. No silent battles. No mind-reading. Just two people showing up, being real, even when it's tough. That's how we grow both as individuals and as a team. And believe me, those hard conversations? They don't drive us apart. They bring us closer.

Donald: You've got to lean into the discomfort sometimes. That's where the growth is. You don't build something strong by skipping over the cracks. You fix them together.

Colleen: So, here's the takeaway: the strongest kind of love, whether it's with your partner, your kids, or your family and friends, is when honesty meets real understanding. Keep your heart wide open, speak the truth with kindness, and stay steady with your love.

Donald: Love's not about having it all figured out. It's about sticking around, telling the truth, and choosing each other even when it's messy. When you've got someone who brings clarity and heart to the table, love doesn't just endure. It flourishes.

Patience and Self-Discipline in a Man's Role

Let's discuss two underrated yet powerful traits every man should master: Patience and self-discipline. These aren't just virtues that wise older men preach about; they're the backbone of strength, success, and respect. Real men stand apart in a world that glorifies instant gratification and quick wins because they understand the value of waiting, working, and staying steady when life throws curveballs.

Let's be honest: Patience and self-discipline aren't exactly the most exciting words in a man's vocabulary. They don't scream adventure, Power, or success. They don't come with instant gratification, and they sure don't make you the life of the party. But if you aim to be a true gentleman, the kind of man who commands respect without demanding it, who moves through life with purpose and grace, then Patience and self-discipline aren't optional. They're essential.

Now, I'm not here to give you a lecture. I'm here to have a conversation. Because the truth is, mastering Patience and self-discipline isn't about losing yourself; it's about refining yourself. It's about tapping into the best version of who you are, not just for the world to see but for your sense of honour, strength, and legacy.

The Power of Patience: It's Not Just About Waiting
When most men hear the word patience, they picture a man sitting quietly, waiting for something to happen, maybe waiting in line, waiting for the right moment, waiting for a woman to text back. But Patience is not passive. It's strategic. It's the ability to control your impulses and emotions so that you don't make decisions that sabotage your future.

Think about it. How many men have ruined relationships, careers, or opportunities because they lacked Patience? A heated argument leads to a breakup. A moment of frustration leads to quitting a job. An impulsive decision leads to regret. The true gentleman understands that Patience is not about inaction but control.

Ever heard the phrase, "Good things come to those who wait"? Cliché, I know. But here's the deal: it's true. Patience is about understanding that effort and consistency will pay off. It's about resisting the urge to quit when things don't go your way. Remember, the journey may be long, but the destination is worth it.

Think about the greats: athletes, people in business, leaders. None of them achieved their current status overnight. Michael Jordan didn't just walk onto a court and become a legend. He was cut from his high school team before he became the icon we admire today. That rejection could have broken him, but his patience and self-discipline turned his failure into motivation.

Whether starting a business, improving your fitness, or working towards a personal goal, Patience keeps you from throwing in the towel when progress feels slow. The ability to endure frustration without making impulsive decisions separates strong men from weak ones. Remember, every step you take, no matter how small, is a step toward your growth and success.

Patience separates the man who reacts from the man who responds. The one who reacts acts on impulse, ruled by his emotions, ego, and fleeting desires. But the one who responds? He takes a breath, weighs his options, and understands the bigger picture. And because of that, he wins in the long run.

Patience in Relationships
Let's discuss patience in relationships, as many men struggle with it. Have you ever heard the saying, "A woman tests a man not because she wants him to fail, but because she wants to see if he's worth trusting"? Powerful, intelligent women don't just give their trust away. They want to see if you can handle pressure, stand firm when things get emotional, and stay calm when they need reassurance.

Patience in relationships is about understanding that not everything needs an immediate fix. It's about knowing that sometimes, she needs you to listen instead of offering solutions. It's about realizing that love is built over time, not in a single grand gesture. A man with patience doesn't rush commitment but doesn't fear it.

He doesn't pressure a woman to move faster than she's ready for, but he also doesn't waste years without purpose. He builds, nurtures, and leads, not forcefully but with presence. Remember, Patience is the key to understanding and strengthening your relationships.

Self-Discipline: The Backbone of a True Gentleman
If Patience is about control over time, self-discipline is about power over self. And let's be honest, this is where most men struggle. Because self-discipline isn't natural, it goes against the grain of every easy, convenient, and pleasurable thing in life.

A man without self-discipline is a slave to his urges. He eats whatever he wants, even when it makes him sluggish and unhealthy. He spends recklessly and then wonders why he's always struggling financially. He chases instant gratification through laziness, distractions, or meaningless relationships, never realizing that real success comes from consistency, not convenience.

A man with self-discipline, though? He's on another level. He doesn't let temporary emotions dictate permanent decisions. He understands the value of sacrifice. He's the man who wakes up early when he'd rather sleep in. Who says no to distractions when he has a goal in mind? Who holds himself accountable, even when no one is watching?

Self-Discipline in Leadership

Every man leads in some way. Leadership requires discipline, whether leading a business, a family, a relationship, or simply leading oneself. A disciplined man doesn't just dream; he executes. He doesn't just talk; he delivers. He understands leadership isn't about barking orders but setting an example.

A disciplined man doesn't just dream; he executes. He doesn't just talk; he delivers. He understands leadership isn't about barking orders but setting an example.

Self-discipline in leadership means:

- Mastering your emotions is a key aspect of self-discipline in leadership. Don't let anger, frustration, or insecurity dictate how you interact with others. Stay composed, setting a positive example for those you lead.
- Committing to personal growth: You're always learning, improving, and pushing yourself to improve.
- Taking responsibility: No excuses. No blaming others. A disciplined man owns his mistakes and learns from them.
- The Balance: How Patience and Self-Discipline Work Together
  Here's where things get interesting. Patience and self-discipline are two sides of the same coin. You need both.
- Self-discipline: Keeps you moving forward even when things get hard. Patience reminds you that the reward is worth the wait. Self-discipline requires showing up daily, even when you don't like it. Patience reminds you that progress takes time. Self-discipline motivates you to develop your character. Patience helps you trust the process.

When these two forces work together, a man becomes unstoppable. He doesn't fall into the traps that take other men down: rage, recklessness, regret. He's steady, strong, and intentional.

The "MR" Factor's Gentleman's Code:

Patience + Self-Discipline = Power

Patience is Power. It's not weakness, passivity, or the ability to wait for the right moment and trust that your efforts will pay off. Self-discipline is freedom. The more you control yourself, the less the world controls you. The more disciplined you are, the more options you create for yourself.

A true gentleman master's both. He is neither impulsive nor passive. He is neither reckless nor afraid. He moves with wisdom, and because of that, he commands respect. Women respect a man who can control his emotions and desires. Employers trust a man who stays committed even when things get tough.

Friends admire a man who doesn't cave under pressure. When you master these two traits, you become unstoppable. You don't just react to life; you shape it. You don't just chase dreams; you make them happen.

You don't have to be perfect. No man is. But if you strive to improve and push yourself to develop Patience and self-discipline, you're already ahead of the game. And that's what separates the boys from the men. So, gentlemen, *The "MR" Factor* isn't about being the loudest, the strongest, or the richest. It's about mastering the art of Patience and self-discipline, the foundation of every great man. So, the question is: Are you ready to take the next step?

Handling Criticism & Learning from Mistakes

Alright, gentlemen. Let's talk about criticism that every man, no matter how confident, accomplished, or self-assured, will face at some point in life. Criticism separates the boys from the men. Criticism is unavoidable, whether it comes from a boss, a partner, a friend, or even a stranger on the internet who thinks they're an expert on everything.

Nobody likes being told they're wrong, especially when they've put their heart and soul into something. But here's the truth: you handle criticism, and learning from mistakes says more about your character than anything else. But here's the real question: How do you handle it? Do you shrug it off, lash out, or take it as a lesson?

The Gentleman's Perspective on Criticism

A true gentleman knows that criticism isn't the enemy. It's an opportunity. And if there's one thing, *The "MR" Factor* teaches, it's that being a man of honour, respect, and self-improvement means mastering the art of taking criticism like a pro, using it as fuel to improve, and turning mistakes into stepping stones for success.

Rule #1: Don't React, Respond: When someone criticizes you, your instinct might be to snap back with a clever rebuttal. But a real gentleman pauses before responding. Take a breath. Absorb what's being said. Then, instead of reacting emotionally, respond with thoughtfulness. A simple phrase like, "That's an interesting perspective.

Can you elaborate?" can work wonders. It shows that you're open to feedback and willing to listen without immediately conceding that the other person is right. By staying composed, you gain respect, whether the criticism is fair or not.

Rule #2: Separate Ego from Improvement: The ego is the enemy of growth. You'll never improve if your pride hurts whenever someone critiques you. The most successful men in history, whether in business, sports, or relationships, could take a hit, learn from it, and come back stronger. Let's say your boss tells you that your presentation lacked clarity. Instead of sulking, ask yourself, "What can I do better next time?"

If your partner tells you they don't feel heard, instead of arguing, consider, "How can I improve my communication?" The ability to put your ego aside and focus on self-improvement is what makes a man truly respectable.

Rule #3: Learn to Filter Feedback: Not all criticism is valuable. Some people criticize others, while others provide more detailed feedback about their issues. A gentleman learns to distinguish between constructive criticism and unnecessary negativity.

A good way to determine if criticism is worth considering is to ask:
- Is this coming from someone who genuinely wants to see me improve?
- Is there truth in what they're saying, even if I don't like hearing it?
- Can I use this information to make myself better?

If the answer is yes, take the feedback to heart. If not, let it roll off your back and move forward.

Rule #4: Turning Mistakes into Lessons: Nothing screams maturity like a man who can say, "I messed up, and I'm working on it." There are no excuses, no blaming others, and no dodging accountability; it's just pure ownership. A true gentleman doesn't see mistakes as failures but as lessons.

Think about it. Some of the greatest men in history have failed frequently. Here are eight greats that come to mind:

1. Abraham Lincoln – Lost numerous elections, failed in business, suffered a nervous breakdown. Became the 16th President of the United States and led the country through its Civil War. He didn't let populace defeat or define his worth.

2. Steve Jobs – Ousted from Apple at age 30 after a power struggle. Returned to Apple and transformed it into the world's most valuable company. Jobs used emotional clarity and vision to reinvent himself and the industry.

3. Nelson Mandela – Branded a criminal and spent nearly three decades in prison. Became President of South Africa and a global symbol of peace and resilience. His ability to forgive and unite was refined in the crucible of hardship.

4. Dwayne "The Rock" Johnson – Cut from the CFL (Canadian Football League), had just $7 to his name. Became one of the highest-paid actors in Hollywood and built a business empire. He took control of his narrative and rebuilt brick by brick.

5. Thomas Edison – Said to have failed 1,000 times before inventing the light bulb. Created revolutionary inventions and shaped modern life. He believed every failure was one step closer to success.

6. Howard Schultz (Starbucks) – More than 200 investors turned him down when he tried to expand Starbucks. Built a global coffee empire. He stuck to his vision with class, honour, and relentless persistence.

7. Walt Disney – Fired from a newspaper job for "not being creative enough," faced bankruptcy multiple times, and had a string of failed businesses. Created the Disney empire, built history's most iconic entertainment brand, and inspired generations. He turned ridicule into resilience and let vision, not ego, guide him forward.

8. Denzel Washington – Flunked out of college with a 1.8 GPA. He was told he'd never make it in Hollywood. Early auditions often ended in rejection. Became a two-time Academy Award winner, a director, and one of the most respected men in film, known for integrity, humility, and wisdom. He didn't let failure define him. He let purpose refine him. He proves that a true gentleman rises through faith, focus, and fearless effort.

Their secret? They didn't let mistakes define them. They used them as stepping stones.

Let's break it down:

- **Own It:** Nothing makes a man look weaker than deflecting blame. If you make a mistake, acknowledge it. A simple "I take full responsibility for that. It won't happen again" shows maturity and integrity.
- **Analyze It:** Ask yourself, What led to this mistake? Was it a lack of preparation, poor judgment, or bad timing? Identifying the cause helps prevent it from happening again.
- **Make Adjustments:** Knowledge is useless without action. If you learn from a mistake but don't apply that lesson, you're doomed to repeat it.

A secret weapon every gentleman should have is a good sense of humour. Learning to laugh at your mistakes takes the sting out of them and keeps you from taking life too seriously. No one gets it right all the time, and that's okay.

What matters is how you handle the moments when you don't. If you trip up, own it, smile, and move forward. Confidence isn't about never making mistakes; it's about not letting them shake you.

Rule #5: Criticism in Relationships: Let's get real about handling criticism from your partner, which can be the trickiest part. Many men get defensive when their significant other points out an issue. But a gentleman listens, even when it's uncomfortable.

Instead of saying, "You're always complaining," try saying, "I hear what you're saying. How can we work on this together?" It's a slight shift, but it makes all the difference. Relationships thrive on communication and a willingness to grow together.

Rule #6: The Gentleman's Approach: Ultimately, how you handle criticism and mistakes is a direct reflection of your character. A real man doesn't shy away from feedback; he welcomes it. He doesn't crumble under the mistakes he learns from them. And he doesn't let his ego stop him from becoming the best version of himself.

So, the next time someone gives you feedback, remember:

- Stay cool, not defensive.
- Filter out the useless from the useful.
- Own your mistakes like a man.
- Respond with class, not combat.
- Use every lesson to grow.
- Keep a sense of humour.

The next time you face criticism, take a deep breath and ask yourself, "How can I use this to improve?" Because that's what being a gentleman is all about. A true gentleman understands that every critique and every misstep is another step toward greatness. So, my friends, stay sharp and humble because that is *The "MR" Factor* in action.

The Importance of Humility and Gratitude: Let's be honest: being a man in today's world is no easy feat. The pressure to succeed, be intense, and have all the answers is relentless. Society expects men to be confident, assertive, and always in control. And while there's nothing wrong with ambition and strength, a quiet power often gets overlooked: Humility and Gratitude.

These two traits, often dismissed as soft or secondary, are, in reality, the foundation of true greatness. They separate the man who demands respect from the one who naturally earns it. They distinguish the man who chases status from the one who commands admiration without trying. And more than anything, they define the kind of gentleman that *The "MR" Factor* seeks to cultivate.

Humility and Gratitude are not just virtues; they are absolute game-changers. They can transform any man who wants to step up, stand out, and make a lasting impact. Let's examine why these two pillars are essential for success, leadership, personal fulfillment, and mastering *The "MR" Factor.*

The Misconception of Humility: A lot of men hear the word Humility and immediately think of weakness. They picture a timid guy who shrinks back, avoids the spotlight, and lets the world walk all over him. But that's not Humility. That's insecurity. True Humility isn't about thinking less of yourself;

it's about thinking of yourself less while remaining secure in your worth.

A humble man doesn't need to prove himself in every conversation. He doesn't need to be the loudest in the room or the one with the last word. A humble man knows that his worth isn't measured by the amount of attention he receives, but by the value he brings to others. He listens, he learns, and he leads without arrogance. And ironically, that's the kind of man people naturally respect and admire.

Why Humility Makes a Man More Influential? People Trust a Humble Man: No one likes a know-it-all. A humble man earns trust because people see he's not trying to prove something. He's trying to improve something. He's open to feedback, willing to learn, and, most importantly, ready to admit his mistakes. That makes him a leader people can count on, providing security and confidence.

Humility Keeps You Growing: When a man believes he has "arrived," he stops evolving. Humility keeps you hungry, striving, and open to opportunities that arrogance would make you blind to.

It Strengthens Relationships: Humility is the glue that holds connections together, whether in friendships, romantic relationships, or business partnerships. A man who listens values others' perspectives, and isn't afraid to say, "I was wrong," will always be respected and appreciated.

It Commands Respect Without Demanding It: The loudest guy in the room may get attention, but the man who carries himself with quiet confidence and genuine Humility is the one who earns lasting respect. Men who demand respect often fail to receive it. Many men hear the word 'humility' and mistake it for weakness. "Why should I be humble? Doesn't that mean letting people walk all over me?" No. True Humility isn't about being a doormat. It's about understanding your worth without constantly having to prove it.

The Confidence in Saying, "I Don't Know": There's a quiet power in admitting when you don't know something. A man who lacks Humility will fake his way through a conversation, pretending to be the smartest in the room. A man with Humility will say, "That's interesting; I don't know much about that, but I'd love to learn." And guess what? That makes people want to teach him, share with him, and invite him into deeper conversations.

The ability to acknowledge when you don't have all the answers doesn't make you less of a man; it makes you better. Learning never stops, and the strongest men are the ones who recognize that growth is a lifelong journey.

The Secret to a Fulfilled Life and the Key to Success: Gratitude is Humility's best friend. It's the secret weapon of a truly fulfilled man. It's the key to success, and it keeps you grounded. It reminds you that no matter how much you achieve, you didn't do it alone. When a man starts believing he has reached his current position solely because of his talent, hustle, or brilliance, he begins to lose touch with reality.

Every success story is built on the shoulders of others: mentors, friends, family, opportunities that were given, and lessons that were learned. A man who recognizes this lives in a state of appreciation rather than entitlement. And here's the secret: Gratitude attracts more of what you appreciate.

Gratitude changes how a man carries himself. It's not just about saying "thank you" when someone opens the door. It's an attitude, a way of living that affects how you interact with people. When you're grateful, you treat others respectfully, not as stepping stones. You acknowledge the small wins, the struggles that shaped you, and those who stood by you.

Gratitude makes life richer. It's easy to chase more money, status, and recognition. But you'll never truly be satisfied if you don't appreciate what you already have. The richest man isn't the one with the most in his bank account. It's the one who can look around at his life and say, "I am grateful for this life, and I will walk through it with humility."

Why Gratitude Elevates a Man's Life

Gratitude Makes You Happier - Science backs this up: grateful men are happier. When a man appreciates what he has instead of always focusing on what he lacks, he finds more joy in everyday life. Happiness isn't about having more; it's about appreciating what you have.

It Makes You More Attractive: Ever notice how people are drawn to those who radiate positivity? That's the power of Gratitude. A man who constantly complains, focuses on what's missing, or acts entitled is exhausting to be around. But a man who genuinely appreciates life, values others, and expresses Gratitude? That's the kind of energy people want in their lives.

It Strengthens Your Connections: Showing Gratitude strengthens relationships, whether with a partner, family, friends, or colleagues. A simple "I appreciate you" goes a long way in making people feel valued. And when people feel valued, they give their best in return.

It Builds Mental Strength: Life isn't always easy. There will be setbacks, failures, and challenges. But a man with Gratitude doesn't dwell on what went wrong. He focuses on what he's learned, how he's grown, and what he still has. That mindset is what separates those who crumble from those who conquer.

The Gentleman's Formula:

Confidence + Humility + Gratitude = The "MR" Factor

Let's put it all together. A man with *The "MR" Factor* is:

- Confident - He knows his worth but doesn't need to prove it.
- Humble - He seeks to learn, grow, and lift others up.
- Grateful - He values what he has and the people around him.

This is the man who commands respect without force. This is the man who earns loyalty and admiration. This is the man who, when he walks into a room, people don't just notice him; they feel his presence.

How The "MR" Factor Cultivates Humility and Gratitude in a Man

The "MR" Factor isn't about turning men into something they're not. It's about refining what's already within them, elevating their potential, polishing their presence, and helping them become men of substance. And what are two qualities that define a man of substance? Humility and Gratitude.

Here's how The "MR" Factor encourages these traits:

- **Teaching the Art of Self-Reflection:** A true gentleman isn't afraid to look inward. Through mentorship and self-awareness exercises, *The "MR"*

Factor helps men recognize their strengths and areas for growth, reinforcing the power of Humility.

- **Instilling the Habit of Appreciation:** Whether through daily gratitude journaling, verbal acknowledgments, or acts of kindness, *The "MR" Factor* ensures that men practice appreciation until it becomes second nature.

- **Encouraging Service to Others:** There's no better way to cultivate Humility and Gratitude than serving others. Whether through mentorship, charity, or simply being a man of integrity in everyday interactions, giving back reinforces these essential qualities.

- **Developing Emotional Intelligence:** A gentleman isn't just well-dressed; he's emotionally intelligent. *The "MR" Factor* emphasizes the importance of understanding others, fostering empathy, and recognizing that authentic leadership isn't about dominance but influence.

The "MR" Factor isn't about status or appearance; it's about character. Nothing defines a man's character more than his ability to remain humble in success and grateful in all circumstances.

The "MR" Factor isn't just about being a man; it's about becoming a better man. And Humility and Gratitude are at the core of that journey. They don't make you weak; they make you stronger. They don't diminish your confidence; they enhance it. A man who masters Humility and Gratitude doesn't just elevate his own life; he uplifts those around him. He leads with quiet confidence; commands respect without demanding it and walks through life with a presence that speaks louder than any title or bank account ever could. The foundation of actual influence, the kind that lasts beyond money, beyond titles, beyond fleeting successes, is Humility and Gratitude.

So, if you want to be a man of influence who effortlessly earns admiration, the kind of man who stands out, not just in appearance but in substance, start here. Carry yourself with Humility. Live with Gratitude. And watch how the world responds.

GENTLEMAN'S GUIDE TO RELATIONSHIPS

Being a Respectful and Supportive Partner
Be honest: being a good partner isn't rocket science, but it takes effort, awareness, and, most importantly, respect. *The "MR" Factor* is all about embodying what it means to be a gentleman, and at the core of that is how you treat your partner.

Forget outdated stereotypes and surface-level charm; genuine respect and support in a relationship go beyond opening doors and picking up the check (though, those gestures don't hurt). It's about consistency, emotional presence, and being a man of integrity.

So, what does it mean to be a respectful and supportive partner? It's not about grand romantic gestures (though those are delightful). It's about the everyday actions that build trust, the small moments that strengthen your bond, and the mindset that makes your partner feel valued, heard, and safe. Keep reading if you want to level up in love and become a man who leaves a lasting, positive impact.

Respect Starts with Awareness
Respect isn't just about treating your partner well when things are easy; it's about how you act when things get tough. Do you

listen without interrupting? Do you acknowledge their feelings, even when you don't fully understand them? Do you hold yourself accountable when you mess up?

Respect is about being aware of your words and actions and how they impact the person you care about. It's about making them feel seen and valued, not dismissed or belittled. It's easy to respect someone when you agree with them, but true respect shows up when you don't. It means you can have hard conversations without shutting down, reacting defensively, or making it all about you.

Let's talk about tone because tone can turn a simple question into a loaded attack. "What's wrong?" genuinely concerned is different from saying, "What's wrong now?" with an exasperated sigh. The first invites conversation, and the second builds walls. Respect is in the details.

Support Isn't Just Words - It's Actions
It's easy to say, "I support you." It's harder to show it in ways that matter. A supportive partner doesn't just nod and say, "That's great, babe," when their partner shares a dream or struggle. They get involved, ask questions, and find ways to make life easier.

Support looks different for everyone. If your partner is starting a new job and feeling overwhelmed, support might mean making sure they have a quiet space to decompress or handling a few extra household tasks so they can focus. If they're chasing a dream, support means believing in them when they doubt themselves. If they're having a bad day, support might mean sitting with them silently without trying to "fix" everything.

A great partner doesn't just cheer from the sidelines; they step onto the field when needed. They're not just there for the wins but for the long nights, the self-doubt, and the times when the world feels heavy.

Communication: The Backbone of Respect and Support
You can't be a truly respectful or supportive partner if you don't communicate well. And no, that doesn't just mean talking; it means listening. It means paying attention to what is being said and also to what is not being said. It means checking in, even when everything seems fine, because you don't wait for problems to arise before you show up.

Good communication isn't just about avoiding arguments, but also about deepening connections. It's about being open, honest, and vulnerable. A real man isn't afraid to express his feelings or ask his partner about theirs. And here's the deal: good communication also means knowing when to shut up. Sometimes, your partner doesn't need a solution; they need space to vent. If you don't know which one they need, ask:

"Do you want advice or just someone to listen?" That one question can prevent half the arguments couples have.

Independence and Interdependence: The Balancing Act
A supportive and respectful partner understands the balance between independence and togetherness. You're a team, but that doesn't mean you must be attached at the hip. Healthy relationships thrive when both people have their own identities, passions, and lives outside of the relationship.

Supporting your partner also means encouraging them to do things for themselves, grow, have friendships, and pursue their interests. It means being secure enough to give them space without seeing it as a threat. Clinginess isn't romance; it's insecurity in disguise.

At the same time, interdependence is key. It means you're there for each other when it matters most. You're reliable, consistent, and trustworthy. You show up, not just because you should, but because you genuinely want to.

Respect in Conflict: The True Test of Character

Anyone can be a great partner when things are going well, but what about when conflict arises? That's when respect is truly tested. It's easy to say "I love you" when the sun is shining; it's harder when you're frustrated, disappointed, or hurt.

Being a respectful partner means arguing in a reasonable manner. It means not resorting to name-calling, gaslighting, or dragging up past mistakes to "win." It means taking a deep breath before you say something you'll regret. It means recognizing that your partner is not your enemy, even when disagreeing.

Here's a golden rule: Pause before reacting. If you feel heated, take a step back. Say, "I need a minute to process this." That simple move can save relationships.

Consistency Over Perfection

Nobody is perfect. You're going to mess up. You're going to say the wrong thing. You will have moments when you're not the best version of yourself. What matters is what you do after. Do you apologize sincerely, or do you make excuses? Do you acknowledge where you went wrong, or turn it around on your partner?

Respect and support aren't about being flawless; they're about being consistent. It's about showing up every day to be your best partner.

The Gentleman's Promise

Being a respectful and supportive partner is a commitment. It's not something you do only when you feel like it; it's something you personify daily. It's in the way you listen, the way you encourage, the way you show up. It's in how you treat your partner, not just in public but behind closed doors.

A true gentleman doesn't just make his partner feel loved; he makes them feel safe. He doesn't just say, "I respect you," but he proves it through his actions.

So, if you want to master *The "MR" Factor* and be the kind of partner that stands out, start with this: Be the man you want your daughter, sister, or best friend to be with. Adjust if your actions wouldn't make you proud in that scenario.

Respect isn't a favour; it's a standard. Support isn't an obligation; it's an honour. And being a great partner? That's the mark of a true gentleman.

The "MR" Factor in Action

Imagine this - Your partner walks in after a tough day, frustration written all over her face. She drops her bag and sighs, and you can tell she's carrying the world's weight.

Option A: You half-listen while scrolling through your phone, muttering something about "That sucks, babe."

Option B: You put your phone down, pull her in for a hug, and say, "Tell me everything."

The "MR" Factor is always about choosing **Option B**. It's about showing up when she needs you, respecting her enough to be present, and supporting her in big and small ways.

Being a respectful and supportive partner isn't just about what you do; it's about who you are. When you embody *The "MR" Factor*, you don't just earn respect; you command it. And trust me, a man like that? That's the kind of man who never has to question whether he's valued because his actions speak louder than words.

So, gentlemen, the challenge is simple: Are you the man who lifts, listens, and loves with strength and purpose? If not, there's no better time to start than right now.

Understanding the Balance of Strength and Vulnerability
Let's discuss something often misunderstood: the intersection of strength and vulnerability. The world might tell you that being a man means showing nothing but strength: muscles, confidence, and grit. We're conditioned to believe that vulnerability is a weakness, a crack in the armour. But here's the truth: strength isn't just about being tough. It's about understanding and accepting both your strength and your vulnerability.

But here's the truth: it's not about picking one or the other. Real strength lies in understanding the balance between both. And when can you do that? Your romantic, professional, and personal relationships become deeper, more genuine, and far more fulfilling. So, let's break it down. Strength and vulnerability aren't opposing forces. They're the perfect pair. In your professional life, vulnerability can lead to stronger connections with colleagues, more effective teamwork, and even career advancement.

Yes, you read that right. Strength and vulnerability can coexist, and when they do, they create a depth in your character that makes you a better partner and person overall. Let's explore why mastering this balance is key to becoming the man you're meant to be and how it'll help you lead a more authentic life.

The Myth of the Invincible Man
Society's idea of "manhood" has been pretty one-dimensional for years. A real man is strong, unshakable, and never afraid to face challenges. Here's a reality check: Unbreakable doesn't mean you're powerful. Strength isn't about walking around like a wall, devoid of emotion or weakness. True strength is having the courage to accept vulnerability. It's facing your fears, flaws, and imperfections without backing down.

Let's think briefly: What do we admire in the people we respect the most? It's often not their sheer power or stoic silence; they can be honest with themselves and others. The ones who admit when they don't have it all figured out but still move forward with confidence.

Vulnerability: Not the Same as Weakness
Let's clear up a huge misconception: vulnerability is not weakness. At all. It's one of the most powerful things you can do as a man. Vulnerability is about showing up as your authentic self without pretending or putting on a facade. It's the courage to admit when you're struggling, share your fears, express your emotions, and trust someone else with your heart.

Vulnerability isn't about breaking down or falling apart; it's about being human. It's about showing the world you're unafraid to be authentic. And it's okay if this feels uncomfortable at first. It's a process, and it's worth it.

When you allow yourself to be vulnerable, you're permitting yourself to connect on a deeper level with the people around you. You're allowing them to see the man behind the tough exterior who has dreams, doubts, insecurities, and hopes. This authenticity builds trust and intimacy, especially in romantic relationships. A woman wants to know that she can rely on you to be her protector and that you are open, honest, and willing to show her who you are.

Strength and Vulnerability: Not Oil and Water
There is a common misconception that vulnerability means weakness. But that's a total myth. Vulnerability isn't about being fragile; it's about being honest and open with yourself and others. It's about allowing yourself to be seen, truly seen, for who you are. And when you do that, you're showing immense strength.

Think about this: A man who can admit feeling insecure, scared, or uncertain is far more resilient than someone who hides those emotions behind invincibility. Why? Being honest with your feelings allows you to face them head-on. You can't conquer what you don't acknowledge. Strength doesn't come from hiding your fears or weaknesses but from confronting them and standing tall.

To be truly strong, you've got to allow yourself to be vulnerable. And when you do that, you become more connected to your feelings and others. And that connection? It builds trust, loyalty, and a deeper bond in your relationships.

The Power of Emotional Honesty
Let's talk about relationships for a minute. Whether you're with a partner, a friend, or a colleague, the ability to communicate openly and honestly about your emotions is a game-changer. It might feel uncomfortable to share your struggles or admit when things aren't going well.

But here's the thing: the more emotionally honest you are, the stronger your relationships will become. This emotional honesty is not a sign of weakness but a display of strength that makes you more secure and resilient. Being vulnerable doesn't mean spilling all your secrets or constantly unloading your emotional baggage. It means being honest when it counts. Instead of bottling up your feelings, let your partner know when you feel overwhelmed.

Share your worries, dreams, and hopes for the future. When you let your guard down and allow your true self to shine through, you invite your partner to do the same. When can you both be authentic with each other? That's when real intimacy begins.

The key is to recognize that vulnerability isn't a sign of weakness. It's a show of courage. It takes strength to trust someone enough to let them see the real you. And when that trust is reciprocated? That's where the magic happens. This courage to trust and be trusted opens up new possibilities and deeper connections.

The Power of Being Both Strong and Vulnerable

Here's the magic formula:

Strength + Vulnerability = Powerful Connection.

Sounds contradictory. But when you understand how to balance the two, you become unstoppable.

1. Strength in the Face of Adversity
Let's face it, life is full of challenges. Whether it's personal struggles, work stress, or relationship hiccups, we all face hard times. But here's where strength comes in: the ability to keep moving forward, even when things are tough.

It's facing adversity head-on and not letting it break you. But here's the twist: being strong doesn't mean you have to do it alone. It's okay to admit that you're having a tough time and to lean on others when you need support. That's where vulnerability shows up in its most powerful form.

Being strong means being able to ask for help when you need it. Knowing that you don't always have to carry the world's weight on your shoulders. When you're vulnerable enough to ask for assistance or share your struggles, you reveal your most significant strength: the ability to trust, open up, and work through problems with others by your side.

2. *Vulnerability in Relationships*
When it comes to relationships, vulnerability is the key to true intimacy. Many guys think that to be a good partner, they must be the rock who always has the answers and never shows weakness. But the truth is, a relationship thrives on emotional connection.

If you constantly try to be "tough," you risk building a wall between you and your partner. While walls may protect you from hurt, they prevent love from flowing freely. Vulnerability allows for deep, meaningful conversations where you can share your fears, hopes, and dreams. When you open up to your partner, you give her the space to open up to you as well. And guess what? This makes you feel more understood, supported, and closer than ever. Vulnerability creates a safe emotional space where both people can be authentic without fear of judgment.

3. *Vulnerability in Personal Growth*
Here's the thing about strength: it's not static. Real strength comes from being open to growth, change, and self-improvement. And you can't grow if you're not willing to be

vulnerable. You're stuck if you're unwilling to acknowledge areas for improvement.

Being vulnerable with yourself means acknowledging your weaknesses, mistakes, and areas for growth. It's okay to admit that you're imperfect and have flaws and struggles, just like everyone else. This self-awareness is the foundation for personal development, making you more well-rounded and confident.

The Dance Between Strength and Vulnerability
Now that we understand the importance of both strength and vulnerability, how do we strike a balance between the two? Here's the secret: it's all about timing and context.

1. Be Strong When You Need To Be
There are times in life when you need to step up and be the strong one. Strength is essential, whether it's dealing with a crisis, taking responsibility, or being a leader. But remember, strength doesn't mean suppressing your emotions or pretending you've figured it out. It means facing challenges head-on and doing what needs to be done.

2. Be Vulnerable When It Counts
There are also times when you need to let your guard down. In relationships, personal growth, and work situations, vulnerability allows you to connect, grow, and be authentic. It's not about showing weakness; it's about being emotionally intelligent enough to know when it's okay to share your true feelings.

The Bottom Line - Be the Full Package
Gentlemen, understanding the balance of strength and vulnerability is the key to becoming the kind of man who attracts others and builds genuine, lasting connections. It's

about knowing when to be the rock and when to let your guard down. It's about having the strength to face challenges while also having the courage to be vulnerable enough to ask for help and connect with others on a deeper level. You become unstoppable when you find that balance because you're no longer just a man of strength. You're a man of depth, connection, and real emotional power. And that, my friends, is *The "MR" Factor.*

THE LOST ART OF ROMANCE

Colleen: Ah, romance. That five-letter word that either gives you butterflies or indigestion, depending on where you are in your love life. Seriously, it used to mean candlelight and courtship. Now it's all, "Hey, you up?" followed by a burrito emoji.

Donald: You're not wrong. Somewhere along the way, we went from writing heartfelt letters to ghosting each other mid-text. Courting used to mean, "I'm serious about you." Now it means, "I didn't cancel our plans, so that's effort, right?"

Colleen: Exactly! There was a time when romance wasn't bought with roses and chocolates. It was earned. And no, I'm not talking about some princess-in-a-tower, sweep-you-off-your-feet, harp-playing-in-the-background fairy tale. Though full disclosure, I do love a good fairy tale. Please give me a tiara and a talking teacup any day.

Donald: And yet, back then, it was all about effort. Men actually courted women. They showed up. On time. With a clean shirt and everything. They didn't show up with a half-charged phone and a "want to split the bill?" attitude.

Colleen: Yes! Courting meant something. It wasn't fast food. It was a slow-cooked Sunday dinner. It was handwritten notes, not just "wyd?" at 11:47 PM. You actually had to get to know someone.

Donald: And men didn't mind putting in the time. You didn't have to post thirst traps or decode texts like hieroglyphics to figure out if someone was interested. You just knew because he was there. Asking questions. Remembering your favourite flower and opening the car door instead of honking from the curb.

Colleen: Now let's get one thing straight: I'm not talking about the cheesy kind of chivalry where a guy shows up with a boombox outside your window blasting Peter Gabriel. (Although... props to John Cusack. Iconic move.)

Donald: That was peak 80s romance. But what we're really talking about here is something deeper. The kind of connection where you actually listen to each other. Where pursuit isn't a game, it's genuine. Courting is about building something real, not just "vibing" until one of you gets bored.

Colleen: These days, it feels like the bar is on the floor. If someone texts back within the hour and uses punctuation, we're swooning. But let's be honest: we've been settling for half-hearted efforts and calling it connection. We deserve better.

Donald: Absolutely. You don't have to play the "let's see where this goes" guessing game. You can raise the bar. You can be the bar. There's a big difference between dating and courting: it's called intention.

Colleen: So, what's the difference, really? Courting says, "I see something in you, and I'm willing to show up consistently to see where this goes." Dating says, "I'll stick around as long as this is convenient, and you don't catch feelings too fast."

Donald: It's time to bring romance back, not with grand gestures and sappy lines but with honesty, presence, and a little effort. You don't need a magic spell. Just a genuine heart and the guts to mean it.

Colleen: Exactly. So, if you're tired of breadcrumbs, vague texts, and glorified "hangouts," do yourself a favour and ditch the swipe culture for some good old-fashioned effort.

Donald: Because the art of courting isn't dead. It's just waiting for someone bold enough to bring it back in style with confidence, a clean shirt, and maybe, just maybe, a playlist that doesn't include trap beats.

Dating: A Casual Experiment
For instance, in casual dating, you might meet someone at a bar, have a few drinks, and then part ways. In contrast, in a courting scenario, you might plan a thoughtful date, such as a picnic in the park, to get to know the person on a deeper level. Dating, in its modern sense, is pretty laid-back.

It's about determining if two people click well together. The whole point is to test the waters, see what's out there, and have fun. You meet someone, go for coffee, grab dinner, watch a movie or two, and see where it goes. If it doesn't work out, you move on. It's like shopping around until you find what you like. The pressure is off, but the emotional investment is often superficial. While this approach has its place in some stages of life, it usually lacks depth and fails to foster a genuine emotional connection.

In today's society, we're taught that dating should be low-pressure. Keep things light, don't overthink it, and let things unfold naturally. You can go on a few dates with someone, share some laughs, ghost them or let things fizzle out naturally. The problem? We truly lose the chance to connect with others on a deeper level. Too often, both men and women wonder, "Was I seen for who I am or just for a fun night out?"

Courting: Intentional and Purposeful
Now, courting is a whole different ballgame. It's not just about seeing where things go; it's about making a clear, intentional choice to explore a relationship with the possibility of a future together. Courting is about getting to know someone deeply. It's about seeing if your values align, if you're willing to grow together, and if there's a genuinely emotional and spiritual connection. The potential benefits of courting over casual dating include a deeper understanding of your partner, a stronger emotional connection, and a more solid foundation for a long-term relationship.

In a world that moves so fast, courting asks us to slow down and be deliberate. It's rooted in respect, not just for the other person but also for yourself. When someone is courting, their actions are intentional. They are there for more than a good time; they are there because they see potential.

After all, they want to build something meaningful with you. And the best part? You get to know each other without the distractions of casualness. This patience in courting reassures you that you don't have to rush into anything, and that the best things take time.

Think about it: when was the last time you truly courted someone? When was the last time you wrote someone a handwritten note to let them know you were thinking about them? Or did you show up at this special someone's door with flowers for no reason other than to brighten their day? These gestures of intentionality aren't just sweet; they're acts of respect and admiration.

These gestures say, "I see you. I appreciate you. I want to know you, truly." This kind of patience and care is almost revolutionary in a world where instant gratification rules. In a relationship, you are not just a passing interest, but a person of value and respect; this is how you should feel.

Look, I get it. Dating is fun. You get to meet new people, go out for drinks, and enjoy the freedom of seeing who fits into your life. But here's the problem: many of us approach dating with a mentality of "it's all good until it's not." And that's where the magic gets lost. People can get lost in the cycle of having a "good time," but what happens when you start looking for something more serious? Where does that leave you?

In today's world, the term "dating" is often used casually. There is no clear sense of purpose; pursuing a more profound connection usually feels superficial. We forget to ask ourselves: What am I looking for? Am I putting in the effort to show up as the best version of myself? Or do we settle for the next best thing that comes along?

The Modern Struggle: Where's the Romance?
Here's the deal: Today's world doesn't encourage this kind of slow-burn romance. We're all caught up in the hustle and bustle of daily life, checking our emails, managing careers, juggling social media, and fitting in relationships whenever we can.

Convenience reigns supreme. And while there's nothing wrong with convenience, it does leave us missing out on something vital: the art of romance. One of the challenges of courting in the modern world is finding the time and space to truly connect with someone amidst the fast-paced nature of our lives.

Romance isn't about grand gestures or extravagant gifts (though those things can be nice). It's about the small, meaningful acts that show you care. It's about taking the time to learn about someone, their dreams, their fears, and their history. It's about being vulnerable and opening up in ways that allow you to connect on a soul level. It's about slowing down, taking a breath, and remembering that love is not just something to be found in the next swipe, but something to be cultivated and nurtured.

In the modern dating world, we often get caught up in "dating apps" or "speed dating" events, trying to connect in a few minutes or based on a couple of photos. But real romance doesn't work like that. It's not about rushing to find the perfect match. It's about taking time, respecting boundaries, learning about the other person, and letting things unfold naturally, without the pressure of ticking off a list of "must-haves."

We need to go back to making each date count, not just as a way to "fill the time," but as a genuine opportunity to explore what could become something much deeper. That, my friends, is the art of romance.

Bringing Back the Romance – The Gentleman's Way
Alright, let's get something straight. There's a difference between dating and courting, and a gentleman knows the difference. Anyone can swipe right and grab a coffee. But a real one? He shows up with purpose. He's not out here chasing moments. He's building something that lasts.

Let's be clear: this isn't about going full Victorian and penning love letters with a quill. It's about doing things with heart. Courting in the modern world means showing up with intention, not confusion. That's the Master's Pillar, which is being in control of your emotions, focused on your pursuit, and crystal clear about what you want. No more mixed signals. If you're into her, show it with presence, consistency, and class.

You don't have to go broke buying roses every day (though props if you do). But you can show up with a little Aure Chi Pillar, the charm, creativity, and spark that separates you from the average guy. Thoughtful gestures? Game-changer. A post it note that says "thinking of you"? It's way smoother than an overused pickup line. Planning a date around something she said in passing? Aure Chi level: unlocked.

And don't forget the Nobler Pillar respect. This is where the grown men separate from the boys. You're not here to play games or ghost people. You're here to honour time, energy, and boundaries. Respect her space, her pace, and her voice. That's how you build trust. That's how you build something real.

Let's break it down, gentleman-to-gentleman:

1. Be Present: Put the phone down, make eye contact, and listen really hard, not just wait for your turn to speak.

2. Be Consistent: Don't show up one day like Prince Charming and disappear the next. If you're serious, act like it.

3. Offer Thoughtful Gestures: It's not about flashy stuff. It's about meaning. Show her you notice, you listen, and you care.

4. Take Your Time: Don't rush to the finish line. Let things unfold. Be curious, not in a hurry.

5. Be Clear About Intentions: Say what you mean and mean what you say. You're not a mystery novel, so don't make her guess the ending.

6. Respect Boundaries: Courting isn't pushy. It's powerful because it honours her voice and values just as much as yours.

Here's the truth: intentional romance doesn't just make her feel special; it makes you feel grounded. It builds your confidence, strengthens your character, and reminds the world that gentlemen still exist.

Do you want to be the guy who turns heads? The one she talks about to her friends not because you're flashy, but because you're real? Then, step into *The "MR" Factor.*

Master yourself. Move with Aure Chi charm. And carry yourself with Nobler respect. The art of courtship isn't dead. It's just waiting for men like you to revive it with soul, swagger, and sincerity.

The Power of Intentionality
Bringing back the art of courting isn't just about doing the old things the old way. It's about infusing intentionality into your actions and understanding what respecting and valuing someone means. The lost art of romance isn't lost; it's just waiting for someone to revive it with purpose. And that someone could be you. This intentionality in courting gives you a clear purpose and focus on your relationships, making you feel more in control and purposeful.

So, as we wrap up here, remember to be intentional, thoughtful, and patient. Romance isn't about grand gestures alone. It's about showing up, being present, and treating the person you're interested in with respect, care, and patience. When you do that, you will stand out from the crowd and create a connection that goes beyond the surface, and that's where the magic truly happens.

GENTLEMAN - BREAKUP & REJECTION

The "MR" Factor is about being more than just another guy. It's about being the gentleman who's worthy of being remembered. A gentleman who knows the difference between dating and courting and who brings back the lost art of romance, one thoughtful gesture at a time.

The "MR" Factor's Way

Let's talk about something most men don't want to admit they don't always handle breakups or rejection well. And I get it. No one likes to hear, "It's not you, it's me" (when deep down, you know it's you). No one enjoys putting their heart out there only to have it handed back like an unwanted takeout order.

But here's the thing: how you handle breakups and rejection isn't just about saving face in the moment. It's about who you are as a man. It's about character, strength, and self-respect. A true gentleman doesn't just win with grace; he also loses with it. *The "MR" Factor* is all about being the kind of man who stands tall, no matter the outcome.

When rejection or a breakup hits, there are two types of men:

The Boy – He lashes out, takes it personally, and lets his ego do the talking. He might send angry texts, beg for another chance, badmouth his ex, or try to make her jealous. He views rejection as an attack on his worth, and his emotions overwhelm him.

The Gentleman – He takes a deep breath, processes the situation, and respects the other person's decision. He doesn't let his emotions get the best of him, and he doesn't make a scene. Instead, he walks away with dignity, knowing that a relationship that isn't meant for him isn't a loss; it's just redirection.

The difference? Maturity, self-respect, and understanding that rejection isn't the end; it's just part of the journey.

How a man navigates the end of a relationship, or an unreciprocated interest, speaks volumes about his character. It's easy to be smooth when things are going well, but the real test of *The "MR" Factor*, that refined, composed, and honourable way of being, comes when the situation is far from ideal.

So, let's break it down. What separates a gentleman from a boy when handling rejection and breakups?

1. He Accepts Reality Without Bitterness
First, a gentleman does not beg, plead, or make excuses when rejected. He doesn't send endless texts trying to change someone's mind. Why? Because he understands the fundamental truth: that someone's feelings are not an obligation. They are a choice.

If a woman isn't interested, has lost feelings, or doesn't see a future, a gentleman respects that. He doesn't lash out, call her names, or act like she's making the biggest mistake of her life. Instead, he acknowledges the situation with dignity.

That doesn't mean rejection doesn't hurt; it does. But instead of letting bitterness take root, a gentleman sees it as redirection. He understands that rejection isn't about his worth, but rather about compatibility, timing, and circumstance. And if she doesn't know the match, she's not the one for him.

The "MR" Factor Move: If you're turned down, acknowledge it with a simple, "I respect that. I wish you the best." Then, move forward with your head held high.

2. He Never Blames or Seeks Revenge

Playing the blame game is one of men's biggest mistakes after rejection or breakups. Suddenly, she's the villain. The "I wasted my time" speeches start rolling in. Maybe he even tries to make her jealous or "get even."

But a gentleman? He knows better. He never seeks Revenge because that's not power; it's pettiness. True strength is in letting go without resentment.

Here's the reality: sometimes people change. Feelings shift. And that's okay. It's painful but blaming someone for not feeling how you want them to; is unfair and immature.

The "MR" Factor Move: If she chooses to leave, don't make it a war: no harsh words, no social media rants, no childish behaviour. Walk away knowing you gave your best.

3. He Handles His Emotions Without Public Drama

A gentleman knows that emotions are real. Heartbreak isn't just a punch to the gut. It's an entire storm. And yet, how he handles those emotions makes all the difference.

Crying in private? Absolutely. Talking it out with a close friend? Essential. But broadcasting his pain all over social media? Ranting about how "all women are the same" in public? No way.

He understands that emotional control doesn't mean suppressing feelings. It means handling them in a way that doesn't create more damage.

The "MR" Factor Move: Find healthy outlets for heartbreak. Hit the gym, journal, talk to a mentor, or do whatever helps you process without drama.

4. He Leaves the Door Closed Once It's Over
One of the most common pitfalls men fall into after a breakup is leaving the door open.

Texting "just to check in." Answering her calls at midnight. Holding onto false hope that maybe she'll change her mind.

No. A gentleman values himself too much for that. He knows that if a woman truly wanted to be with him, she wouldn't have left in the first place. He refuses to be the backup plan or an emotional safety net.

The "MR" Factor Move: When a breakup happens, he steps back completely. He doesn't beg for closure. He doesn't hang around waiting for breadcrumbs. He moves forward like a man who knows his worth.

5. He Sees Breakups as Lessons, Not Failures
A gentleman understands that every relationship teaches something valuable about himself, love, and wants.

Instead of dwelling on what went wrong, he asks:
- What did I learn about myself in this relationship?
- What qualities do I need in a future partner?
- How can I grow from this experience?

The "MR" Factor Move: Take time after a breakup to reflect. Write down the lessons. Use them to become a better man.

6. He Focuses on Growth, Not Rebound Relationships
After a breakup, many men rush into the next available relationship to fill the void. They start chasing attention, going out of their way to prove they've "moved on."

But a gentleman? He takes his time. He doesn't need a rebound to validate his worth. He understands that healing comes from within, not from the next distraction.

The "MR" Factor Move: Instead of jumping into another relationship immediately, he takes a step back and invests in himself mentally, physically, and emotionally.

7. He Holds His Standards, Even in Heartbreak
Even in pain, a gentleman never lowers his standards. He doesn't let rejection make him bitter toward women. He doesn't let heartbreak turn him into someone cold or cynical.

Instead, he doubles down on being the kind of man who attracts the right relationship, one built on mutual respect, shared values, and genuine connection.

The "MR" Factor Move: Stay true to your standards. Never let one failed relationship make you believe that love isn't worth it.

8. He Walks Away with Gratitude and Respect
No matter how a relationship ends, a gentleman always finds something to be grateful for. Maybe she helped him grow. Maybe she brought laughter into his life. Perhaps she showed him what wasn't right for him.

Instead of focusing on what was lost, he focuses on what was gained. And he moves forward with grace, ready for the next chapter.

The "MR" Factor Move: Say goodbye with gratitude, even if it hurts. Leave the past where it belongs with dignity.

I once dated a guy who was all about the honeymoon phase, the first six months, when everything was butterflies and romance.

One day, he casually mentioned that after decades of dating, he realized it only takes nine months to get over a breakup fully.

And you know what? He wasn't wrong. When we broke up, sure enough, nine months later, I was completely over him. I'm just putting that out there for anyone who needs a heads-up!

The Gentleman's Mindset: Strength in Every Loss

Donald: Guys let's talk real for a minute. Do you know what separates a man from a gentleman? It's not how he wins. It's how he handles the loss. Anyone can smile when life's going great. But when things fall apart? That's when your real character shows up.

Colleen: Truth. Love isn't always a smooth ride. Sometimes the connection fizzles, sometimes she says no, and sometimes you get hit with the dreaded, "It's not you, it's me." And let me tell you, how you act in those moments? That's where your Gentleman Card either gets stamped or revoked.

Donald: A real gentleman doesn't measure his worth by who chooses to stay. He stands on solid ground even when someone walks away. He doesn't bad-mouth her, doesn't beg, doesn't crumble. He nods, respects the moment, and keeps it classy. That's strength, not noise.

Colleen: Exactly. When a man knows who he is, rejection doesn't rattle him. It redirects him. Breakups don't break him. They build him. It's not about pretending it doesn't hurt. It's about choosing not to let that hurt define you.

Donald: So next time a relationship ends, or a woman says, "I don't see us like that," ask yourself: Am I reacting like a boy who didn't get his way or responding like a gentleman who knows his value? That's the difference right there.

Colleen: Because here's the thing: how you handle hard moments, that's the real test. Not the easy days. Anyone can play cool when everything's falling into place. But it takes wisdom, self-control, and maturity to walk away with your head high and your heart intact.

Donald: There's no shame in feeling it. But bitterness? That's a trap. Let it go. Pick up your pride, not your ego. Grow from the experience and level up. You're not defined by who walked away. You're defined by how you rise after they do.

Colleen: And when the right one comes along? She'll recognize that strength. She'll see the way you carry yourself and know she's dealing with a man who's done the work. A man who is the work.

Donald: So go forward. Keep becoming better. Stay rooted in self-respect and carry The "MR" Factor with every step. You don't need to win every heart. Just win back your own when it's bruised.

Colleen: Now that's the gentleman's mindset class in the chaos, strength in every loss, and growth in every goodbye.

EXAMPLES OF A MODERN DAY GENTLEMAN

The Ethics of Success: Modern-Day Gentleman
Success today isn't just about fame or wealth; it also involves purpose, integrity, and impact. The term *"The Three Pillars of a Gentleman" refers to a modern concept of the Master's, Aure Chi, and Nobler within every man that shows a leadership that emphasizes using success to elevate others and redefine what*

leadership entails. Look at six influential men who personify this concept and show us the power of using success for good.

Bill Gates: Defining Traits: Vision and Responsibility

As co-founder of Microsoft and philanthropist through the Bill & Melinda Gates Foundation, Gates has used his immense wealth to tackle global health and education issues. His vision isn't just about profit; it's about changing the world, from eradicating diseases to improving access to education and clean water.

Barack Obama Defining Traits: Grace Under Pressure

As the first Black U.S. president, he navigated complex challenges with resilience, calm, and dignity. Obama's success wasn't just political; his ability to remain composed and focused under immense pressure made him a respected leader whose example of grace continues to inspire.

José Andrés Defining Traits: Compassion and Action

José Andrés, a chef, is a shining example of selflessness. Through World Central Kitchen, he has provided meals to communities in disaster-stricken areas worldwide. His success is measured by how he uses his platform and resources to serve others, showing that compassion can drive impactful change.

David Suzuki Defining Traits: Environmental Stewardship

As an environmental activist, Suzuki has dedicated his life to protecting the planet. He founded the David Suzuki Foundation and raised awareness about climate change and biodiversity. Suzuki's success is defined by his relentless commitment to environmental preservation for future generations.

LeBron James Defining Traits: Giving Back with Purpose

Through his foundation, he's provided scholarships and built the "I PROMISE School" for at-risk youth. Beyond basketball,

LeBron is a fierce advocate for social justice. He uses his influence to allow others to succeed, proving that success is about lifting others and contributing to a fairer world.

Sir Richard Branson Defining Traits: Audacity and Altruism.
As founder of the Virgin Group, he turned bold risk-taking into an art, building ventures across industries from airlines to space. Yet beyond business, his heart-led leadership shines, championing mental health, environmental causes, and social equity through Virgin Unite. Branson's success lies in innovation and in using it to uplift others with purpose and joy.

By focusing on vision, grace, compassion, influence, leadership, and respectful, proving that leadership isn't just about what you achieve but how you use it to elevate others. Let's take inspiration from their stories and redefine your path to success.

Prosperity Without Greed: The Ethics of Success
We all know success is often measured by wealth, but let's get straight: true prosperity isn't about how fat your bank account is. *The "MR" Factor* is about redefining success with a healthy dose of ethics. It's about achieving financial gains and personal and social fulfillment without letting greed take the wheel. Greed is that monster that eats away your integrity, while prosperity comes from honourable ambition.

In today's world, there's a lot of pressure to chase after wealth, no matter the cost. But *The "MR" Factor* flips the script. A true gentleman doesn't crave riches for the sake of it; he creates wealth through intelligence, effort, and ethical choices. *The "MR" Factor* empowers you to understand that prosperity isn't the quickest way to cash in; it's about building something lasting with honour, responsibility, and service.

The Gentleman's Creed: Wealth with Integrity

A man who follows *The "MR" Factor* knows success doesn't come without solid principles. He doesn't cut corners or step on others to get ahead. His word means something, and his wealth reflects his character, not just his paycheck.

Chasing financial success should never come at the cost of your ethics. Greed breeds selfishness, dishonesty, and exploitation. *The "MR" Factor* says no to all that and instead follows the following:

- **Earn With Honour** – If you have to lie or cheat to make money, it's not real wealth. The "MR" man builds a fortune through hard work, creativity, and fair play.
- **Give Without Obligation** – Real prosperity means sharing what you've earned. The "MR" man views wealth as a means to help others, not a trophy to flaunt.
- **Lead With Responsibility** – The "MR" man is a man of success who doesn't hoard power; he uses it to inspire and protect those around him.

True success is sustainable, lasts, and leaves a legacy of respect, not regrets. *The "MR" Factor* is about integrity, not how much stuff you can pile up.

The Poison of Greed

Greed is like a quiet thief. It steals your peace, your principles, and, ultimately, your prosperity. A greedy man is never satisfied. No matter how much he has, he's always hungry for more, and in his quest, he sacrifices his values, relationships, and sometimes even his health.

Look at history: greedy leaders, businessmen, and influencers who had it all but lost everything because they couldn't control their hunger for more. Greed blinds people to the consequences of their actions, making them justify all sorts of unethical choices as *"ambition."*

The "MR" Factor calls greed what it is: a self-destructive force. A gentleman doesn't let money control him; he controls his money. True success isn't about excess; it's about your impact.

The "MR" Factor's Path to Ethical Prosperity
Success doesn't just happen. It's the result of wise, disciplined choices. *The "MR" Factor* provides a roadmap to prosperity without sacrificing your values to greed.

Mastering Financial Wisdom
Money is a tool, not your master. A man who follows *The "MR" Factor* doesn't mindlessly throw away his earnings on foolish things or chase money. He builds financial security through smart decisions and knowledge. He understands:

- The difference between need and want.
- The power of investing rather than spending.
- The importance of ethical business practices.

He earns his money with dignity and manages it with discipline, never compromising his integrity for a quick buck. Instead of looking for shortcuts, he plays the long game, building prosperity that benefits himself and those around him.

Elevating Others Along the Way
Prosperity isn't a solo mission. *The" MR" Factor* teaches that true success is about helping others succeed, too. A man of *The "MR" Factor* lifts the community he mentors, creating opportunities and supporting causes that matter.

Greedy people hoard wealth; prosperous ones circulate it. *The "MR" Factor* man knows that when the tide rises, all boats float. His generosity isn't for recognition; it's for making a real difference.

Defining Success Beyond Wealth
A real gentleman understands that being rich isn't the be-all and end-all. Prosperity includes your health, relationships, character, and purpose. A wealthy man who lacks integrity is poor in all the areas that matter most.

The "MR" Factor welcomes a well-rounded definition of success:
- Personal Growth: A man who's always learning, constantly improving.
- Meaningful Relationships: A man who values love, family, and friendships.
- Purpose-Driven Work: A man whose career reflects his values.

When you measure success holistically, there's no room for greed. Prosperity becomes a fulfilling and meaningful way of life, not just about stacking cash. It's about feeling satisfied and content with your achievements, knowing you've made a positive impact.

The Legacy of Ethical Prosperity
What's the mark a man leaves on the world? Greedy men are remembered for scandals, broken promises, and betrayal. Prosperous men are remembered for their character, their contributions, and the positive impact they made. *The "MR" Factor* ensures that a man's legacy is one of honour. It teaches men to build wealth with integrity so that their name stands for respect, not shame. A gentleman's success story is about how well he lived; not just how much he made.

Time to Choose: The Path of Prosperity or Greed?
Every man has a choice: pursue wealth at any cost or build prosperity with honour. *The "MR" Factor* is all about the second option. It teaches that success comes from integrity, discipline, and balancing ambition with values. Prosperity without greed isn't just possible; it's the only real way to succeed. So, how do you define success? What kind of legacy do you want to leave? The choice is yours.

HOW TO LEAD & INSPIRE OTHERS

The Power of Generosity and Mentorship
You don't need a crown or a corner office to be a leader. Leadership is not reserved for the loudest voice in the room; it belongs to the heart that shows up, gives back, and lifts others higher. Real leadership? It's like being the sunrise after a long night; it brings hope, clarity, and warmth. And the secret power behind it all? Generosity and mentorship. When shared, two mighty forces flow like music in the wind, lifting others, lighting paths, and leaving legacies. Let's discuss how giving back can transform you into the leader others are inspired to follow and the kind of leader you'll be proud to become.

The Match That Lights the Torch
Generosity is not about wealth; it's about spirit. It's the warm coat you wrap around someone when life's weather gets cold. It's the umbrella you offer in a downpour, even if it's your only one. Generosity is how leaders say, "I see you. I've got you."

It doesn't have to be a grand gesture. Sometimes, it's lending your ear when someone needs to talk or sharing your experience so someone else doesn't trip over the same stones. No matter how small, every act of generosity is a pebble tossed into still water; it sends waves. It matters. Do you want to inspire? Be the one who gives without keeping score. Be the one who shows others that there's always enough kindness. When you give, you become a living example that leadership is not about holding power; it's about passing it on.

Be the Bridge, Not the Barrier
Think of mentorship as building a bridge across a canyon someone else is afraid to cross. You've already made the journey. You've stumbled, you've climbed, you've learned. So now you say, "Come on. Walk with me. I'll help you get there."

Mentorship is leadership in its most powerful human form. It's not about having all the answers; it's about walking beside someone as they discover their own. You don't need to be perfect to mentor someone; you must be real. Honest. I will say, "I've been there too, and here's what helped me."

Being a mentor is like being a lighthouse: you're not steering their ship but showing them where the rocks and the open sea lie. That kind of leadership inspires loyalty, growth, and gratitude. And when your mentee starts to soar, that's the reward, the fruit from the tree you helped grow.

Walk It Like You Talk It
Here's the truth: people watch more than they listen. They don't follow your words; they follow your walk. So, if you want to lead and inspire others to give, mentor, and grow, be the walking, talking example. Live the values you preach.

It's like being the first to dance on an empty dance floor. At first, people hesitate, but when they see your joy, courage, and rhythm, they jump in. That's the magic of leading by example. When you lead with generosity and open-hearted mentorship, you don't just influence minds, you awaken spirits. You say with your life: "It's safe to give. It's powerful to care. You can rise by lifting."

Build Circles, Not Thrones
The most powerful leaders don't build empires; they build communities. Giving back doesn't elevate you above others; it gathers people beside you. Mentorship and generosity create circles of strength where everyone feels seen, heard, and supported.

Think of it like a bonfire. When you give back, you're adding wood to a communal flame. That fire warms everyone who comes near it. It doesn't burn out; it blazes bigger. And when others start bringing their logs, the warmth spreads further than you ever imagined. You've created something more than leadership when you create spaces where people feel safe to grow, shine, and stumble. You've created a legacy.

Watch the Garden Bloom
There is no feeling quite like watching someone you've helped thrive. It's like planting a seed and watching it bloom into a field of wildflowers. You see their confidence grow, their dreams take root, and you know, deep down, you helped water that growth.

And guess what? Those you inspire will go on to inspire others. That's how real change happens, not in big speeches, but in one soul touching another. You mentor one. They mentor two. Suddenly, you've sparked a movement, an invisible line of goodness, courage, and compassion connecting countless lives. This is the power of your leadership.

You Were Meant to Inspire
You are more powerful than you know. You don't need to wait for a title to lead. You need to give. To reach out. To lift someone up. Because when you do, you shine. And when you shine, others see the light in themselves. So, be generous with your time, wisdom, and heart. Be a mentor, a friend, and a leader who makes others feel like they can fly.

Because you, dear reader, are not just here to climb mountains. You are here to build trails. To light lanterns. To plant forests. And in doing so, you will become the kind of leader who doesn't just make a difference. You'll make others believe they can, too. Now go. Shine bright. Someone's waiting for your spark.

Becoming a Role Model for the Next Generation
Let's be real; life isn't just about waking up, paying bills, and scrolling through the same old news feed. It's about living with purpose, like a compass pointing north, even when the winds of life try to blow you off course. And when you walk purposefully, you're not just walking for yourself; you're leaving footprints for someone else to follow. Whether you know it or not, you're becoming a living lighthouse for the next generation.

Being a role model doesn't require perfection. It requires presence. It means being a mirror that reflects courage, a lantern in someone else's dark tunnel, and sometimes, just a gentle hand on a trembling shoulder saying, "You got this."

So, how do you live with purpose, create an impact, and become a legacy in motion for the young eyes watching? Let's unpack it together with heart, hope, and a little dose of real talk. Here are the seven living purposes of a role model:

1. Purpose: Is Your Inner Reach, Not a Job Title
The purpose isn't always flashy. It's not written in bold letters across a resume or carved into plaques. It's more like a heartbeat; it's constant, even when you're not thinking about it, that whisper inside nudges you toward something meaningful, something bigger than yourself.

Living with purpose means showing up with intention, even when no one's clapping. It's cooking dinner with love because your family matters. It's time to start that side hustle to fund a cause close to your heart. It's being kind when it's easier to be cold. Purpose doesn't need an audience; it just needs truthfulness. And when the next generation sees you living on purpose, following your inner drumbeat, not the world's noise, they learn to listen to their rhythm, too.

2. Impact Is the Echo of What You Give

You don't need to be famous to make an impact. Some of the loudest echoes come from the smallest, most sincere actions. Think of your life like a pebble tossed into a pond. Every act of kindness, every encouraging word, and every truth you live out creates ripples that go farther than you can see.

When you choose to help someone instead of judging them, you send out waves of inspiration by showing up for a child, a neighbour, or even a stranger. These are the seeds of impact that don't bloom overnight but grow like wildflowers in someone else's soul. You might not see the harvest, but trust this: someone out there will feel your influence and quietly change their course.

3. The Role Model Effect: Watchful Eyes Than You Think

Kids don't need perfect people. They need real people who fall, get up, and keep going. They need to see what resilience looks like with wrinkles, what joy looks like after heartbreak, and what wisdom sounds like without preaching.

Being a role model is less about saying the right things and more about living them. It's showing them how to navigate storms, apologize when they're wrong, and laugh at themselves when life hands them lemons the size of grapefruits. You are the story they'll remember when they face a crossroads. Be the chapter they flip back to when they need courage. Be the voice in their head that says, "I watched them make it through; so, can I?"

4. Purpose Looks Different on Everyone
Living with purpose isn't a one-size-fits-all situation. For some, it's raising strong kids. For others, it's building a business, leading with integrity, healing others, or simply bringing joy like a warm cup of coffee on a cold day.

Don't compare your path to someone else's highlight reel. You might be planting seeds while others are harvesting crops. Trust that your season matters. Walk your purpose like it's tailor-made for you because it is. And remember, even a small and steady candle can illuminate the way for others to see. Your light matters, even when it flickers. Keep shining.

5. Teach Through Living, Not Lecturing
The best lessons are caught, not taught. Let the next generation catch your patience, laughter, ability to forgive, discipline, and belief in second chances. Let them see your humility like a soft breeze, not a hammer.

You don't need a microphone to inspire. Just live so honestly and with such quiet conviction that your life becomes a lesson plan. When they see how you treat waitstaff, bounce back from disappointment, and speak about others behind closed doors, they're taking notes. Make your life one worth studying. And don't be afraid to say, "I messed up, but here's what I learned." That's the real thing that builds trust. That's the kind of honesty that raises warriors.

6. Legacy Isn't Left. It's Lived.
Legacy isn't what you leave when you're gone; it's what you live while you're here. It's how you make people feel, help others believe, and show them what's possible when you stay true to yourself. Think of legacy like a garden you tend to every day. Every conversation, every choice, every moment of grace is a seed. And one day, someone will sit in the shade of your planted

tree. They'll say, "Because of you, I believed I could." That's the impact. That's the purpose. That's being a role model.

7. Small Steps, Big Shifts
You don't need to change the whole world in a day. You need to change someone's world in a moment. Smile more. Share more. Teach more. Show up. Be kind, even when it's not easy. Today's small steps could be the spark that lights a fire in a child, a teen, or a friend stumbling in the dark. The purpose isn't a destination. It's a way of walking. So, walk with courage. Walk with love. Walk as if your footprints matter, because they do.

You Are the Blueprint
Someone is watching how you handle life, hoping to find strength in your stride. Someone younger, unsure, and silently wondering: "Can I make it?" You get to show them the answer, not with a lecture, but with your life. Live with purpose, give with love, grow through your messes, keep rising, keep shining. Be the example you wish you had, or better yet, be the one you're proud to become.

You don't have to be perfect...
- Just present.
- Just real.
- Just you, living on purpose, making your mark.

When you do that, you're not just becoming a role model.

THE "MR" FACTOR MOVEMENT

Donald: Alright, guys, lean in. I know we've covered a lot in this book, but before we wrap this thing up, let's run it back one more time straight, no fluff. Because I don't want you closing this book with question marks. I want you to walk away with bold confidence, clear purpose, and zero confusion about what *The "MR" Factor* is.

Colleen: We're not talking about the old-school version of manhood. You know, the loud one, always puffing its chest, picking fights to prove it's tough. That's not power. That's insecurity in a leather jacket.

Donald: Exactly. Absolute power doesn't need to shout. It doesn't need a spotlight or an audience. It walks in, calm as still water, and somehow, the whole room listens. That's the kind of man *The "MR" Factor* is raising a man who doesn't just talk tough…he is tough in the right ways.

Colleen: He is the kind of man who doesn't get loud because he doesn't need to. His presence says it all. You feel him before he speaks, and when he does, his words carry weight because he's been through fire, and he came out forged, not fried.

Donald: Do you want to know what *The "MR" Factor* is? It's not just a course. It's a calling. It's a movement back to real, grounded, grown-man greatness. A transformation. A rise. A mission to become the kind of man this world needs, not the type it's been tolerating.

Colleen: You're not the guy searching for validation. You're the one standing firm, lighthouse-style, in the middle of a storm. Not chasing attention attracting it. Why? Because you know who you are. And you've done the work.

Donald: *The "MR" Factor* turns you from a question mark into an exclamation point. No more drifting through life like a lost signal. You become a tower broadcasting truth, purpose, strength, and protection for everyone around you.

Colleen: Because here's the deal: a guy gets older, sure. But a gentleman? He grows wiser. He evolves. He learns how to hold space, handle pressure, and live with principle. That's the difference. And that's *The "MR" Factor*.

Donald: Don't let this be another "good read." Let it be your launch pad. You've got the blueprint. Now, it's on you to live it, breathe it, and be it.

Colleen: Because trust us once you step into the real you? Oh, the world's going to notice.

MANHOOD IS LEARNED, NOT INHERITED.

Why the World Needs The "MR" Factor - Because the world is tired of counterfeit courage and emotional confusion, we're craving the kind of men who don't break promises or people and fix things with their hands, hearts, and humility. We're thirsty for leaders, listeners, and lifters. *The "MR" Factor* is where you don't just learn how to lead, but you know why. You don't just evolve; you elevate.

This isn't about becoming someone else but becoming who you are meant to be. Men are being called not to dominate but to demonstrate. Not to impress but to express. Not to rule but to rise. *The "MR" Factor* is the reset button, the clean slate, the blueprint that reminds men:

"Real strength doesn't shout; it echoes in what's done, not said."

Let's be honest; too many men are walking around like Ferraris with no steering wheels. All power, no direction. *The "MR" Factor* gives you the wheel, the map, and the fuel. This isn't a lecture. It's an awakening. This isn't about teaching men how to wear a tie. It's about teaching them how to tie integrity to their identity. It's not just skills. It's substance. It's not hype. It's honour. Chivalry isn't dead; it's just been waiting for a man who remembers who he is.

Being a man in today's world can feel like walking a tightrope over criticism, confusion, and contradiction. But here's the secret: You're not meant to walk it alone. *The MR Factor* is a community, a brotherhood that offers support, guidance, and a shared mission. You're meant to walk tall. *The "MR" Factor* is the wind beneath your stride, the mirror that shows you your royalty, and the map back to your manhood's mission.

One man said it like this: "Before *The "MR" Factor*, I was reacting. Now, I'm responding with wisdom, weight, and purpose."

This is the transformation. Every man has a crown, but not every man knows how to wear it without letting it slip into ego or rust in fear. *The "MR" Factor* teaches you how to wear it with grace, grit, and greatness.

Colleen: Let's get this straight. You are not your past. Not the pain, not the mistakes, and not the names they gave you. You are your next move. You are the man who chooses growth over guilt, strength over shame. You are the apology that heals, the decision that transforms, and the presence that matters.

You don't have to be perfect. But you do have to show up with purpose, grit, and heart. Because your next chapter isn't going to write itself. And trust me: The world is watching, your purpose is waiting, and it's your time.

Donald: Hey, you made it to the end. That says something. It's not just about your commitment to finishing a book but about the kind of man you're ready to become.

Colleen: It also says you're not afraid of growth. And let me tell you, most people want change, but very few are willing to make it happen. So, first off, hats off to you for showing up for yourself.

Donald: Look, this wasn't just a book. It was a conversation between seasoned men, honest and ready to rise. *The "MR" Factor* is about reclaiming what it means to be a gentleman in today's world. And that doesn't mean being perfect. It means being purposeful.

Colleen: Mmm, I really like that part, Sweetie. We're not here to tell you to go back in time. We're here to remind you that respect, self-control, discipline, and character those things never go out of style. They just got a little quiet in all the noise. You, my friend, are the one who brings them back to life.

Donald: Thank you, Sweetheart. Me too. There's a difference between a man who reacts and a man who responds. A man who drifts and a man who leads. The fact that you're still here means you're leaning into the leader you're meant to be.

Colleen: And trust me, we know life will test you. People will doubt you. The world will sometimes misunderstand your quiet strength. But you keep rising. Because a gentleman doesn't need approval, he moves with intention.

Donald: You've read the principles. You've heard the stories. But here's the real question: Are you ready to live *The "MR" Factor*?

Colleen: Because let me tell you, when a man walks with this kind of presence, when he learns how to listen, lead, love, and let go with grace, everything changes. His relationships, his confidence, his peace. And yes, the right woman will feel that without you saying a word.

Donald: We wrote this book not only to teach but also to invite you. Into something higher. Into manhood with meaning. Into a life that's not just lived but led.

Colleen: So, as we close these pages, we're not saying goodbye. We're just saying go walk this out. You've got the wisdom. You've got the tools. Now, go build the legacy.

Donald: From one gentleman to another, carry The "MR" Factor with pride.

Colleen: And remember, true power never has to shout. It simply shows up.

"A man plays the game. A gentleman rewrites the rules, so everyone wins."

Colleen C. Carson

www.ingramcontent.com/pod-product-compliance
Lightning Source LLC
Chambersburg PA
CBHW070817250426
43671CB00037B/2554